TURNING POINTS
IN DYNAMIC PSYCHOTHERAPY

INITIAL ASSESSMENT, BOUNDARIES, MONEY,
DISRUPTIONS AND SUICIDAL CRISES

D1710055

SALMAN AKHTAR

First published in 2009 by
Karnac Books Ltd.
118 Finchley Road
London NW3 5HT

British Library Cataloguing in Publication Data
A C.I.P. is available for this book from the British Library.

ISBN-13: 978-1-85575-681-6

www.karnacbooks.com

To

IRA BRENNER
in friendship

Contents

ACKNOWLEDGMENTS

I am thankful to Michael Vergare, M.D. who, as the Chairman of the Department of Psychiatry and Human Behavior at the Jefferson Medical College, has given my work unwavering support. Many other colleagues have helped in preparation of this book more directly, either by commenting upon earlier drafts of various chapters or by lending me instructive vignettes from their clinical practices. Needing special mention in this regard are Drs. Jennifer Bonovitz, Ira Brenner, Jill McElligot, Jaswant Guzder and Rajnish Mago. Drs. Mark Moore and Robert McFadden provided some very useful references. Dr. Robert Berger pointed out a significant error of citation on my part and thus saved me from later embarrassment. Portions of Chapter One have been taken from my book, *Broken Structures: Severe Personality Disorders and Their Treatment* (Jason Aronson, 1992) and Chapter Four from *Severe Personality Disorders: Everyday Issues in Clinical Practice*, ed. B. van Luyn, S. Akhtar and W.J. Lively (Cambridge University Press, 2007) with the permission of their respective publishers. My secretary, Melissa Nevin, prepared the manuscript with her usual industry and grace. To all these individuals, my sincere thanks indeed.

My wife and fellow psychoanalyst, Dr. Monisha Nayar, typed parts of the manuscript and supported my work in many other ways. By gently pointing out my errors and omissions, she considerably improved its clarity and accuracy. To her, my gratitude is sweet and profound.

INTRODUCTION

Putting aside the narcissistic-masochistic aspiration of authoring a text on all the intricacies of in-depth psychotherapy, I have chosen to address five areas of difficulty in this enterprise. This relatively restricted focus has made it possible to tackle matters in their true complexity and intrigue. The loss of breadth is thus compensated by the gain in depth.

The areas I have chosen to explicate pertain to initial assessment, boundaries, money, disruptions, and suicidal crises. Over three decades of clinical experience has taught me that most problems in the course of dynamic psychotherapy involve these areas; their proper understanding and management is key to productive therapeutic work. Each chapter of this compact book tackles one of these areas in detail, outlining not only the conceptual issues at hand but also the technical strategies that emanate from them.

The first chapter deals with initial assessment. I start with the premise that most psychotherapies fail or come to an impasse because agreement upon goal and method of treatment was not arrived at between the patient and therapist. Consequently, I underscore the necessity of conducting a thorough assessment before the decision to embark on psychodynamic psychotherapy is taken. The assessment interview I delineate is unlike the traditional psychiatric history-taking. It focuses upon three main areas, namely the patient's need for deep psychotherapy, the patient's suitability for such psychotherapy, and the actual feasibility of undertaking a long, drawn-out procedure. In each of these categories I outline further tasks, explain their theoretical basis, and describe the technical means of accomplishing them. I also explain the procedure of making diagnostic clarifications and therapeutic recommendation by putting all this data together. Ground is thus set for the chapter that follows.

Boundaries of the therapeutic frame form the next topic. Instead of providing manualized guidelines, I first discuss the concept of intrapsychic and interpersonal boundaries in detail. I then address matters of optimal distance and attempt to demonstrate how the issue of boundaries and distance affect the therapeutic technique from its inception to its end. I conclude by discussing boundary violations of sexual, aggressive, narcissistic, and cultural types and by offering strategic pointers to avoid slippage in these realms.

The next chapter deals with money since conflicts around it frequently impact upon psychotherapy. I begin with a survey of psychoanalytic writings on the emotional meanings of money. Then, in a novel twist to the existing literature, I offer the description of six psychopathological syndromes involving money: chronic miserliness, inordinate generosity, characterological overspending, bargain hunting, monetary masochism, and pathological gambling. Moving on to the technical side of issues, I discuss the art of setting fees, the role of third-party payers, and the impact of money upon the transference and countertransference developments. I then discuss the special situations involving the treatment of extremely wealthy patients, children and adolescents, and the usually indigent clinic cases. I also elaborate upon the pros and cons of gratis work. I note that while misunderstandings and miscommunications vis-à-vis exchange of money within the clinical dyad lead to difficulties, their exploration provides an opportunity to understand the depth of the patient's symptomatology and subtle characterological ways of operating in life.

My discussion of these mutual misunderstandings easily leads to the chapter on disruptions which can, at times, cause a complete breakdown of collaboration between the patient and therapist. Noticing that such threats to therapeutic alliance have varied etiologies and manifest in different forms, I move on to outlining, in a step by step fashion, the interventions to deal with them. In this context, I elucidate the therapeutic functions of holding and containing, limit-setting, employing adjunct measures, and the need to oscillate one's approach in conjunction with the patient's psychostructural level at a given moment.

I end the book with a chapter dealing with suicidal despair. In it, I discuss the multifactorial etiology of self-destructive intent and action in the hope that awareness of the complex issues underlying them will help therapists better empathize with the patient. I go on to tackle the management of acutely and chronically suicidal patients in depth and also address the thorny matters of emergency room patients with unclear suicidal potential, and patients who make desperate, suicidally-bent, late-night phone calls to their therapists.

Rounding off this thumbnail sketch of its contents, I wish to emphasize four 'tendencies' that run like blood vessels through the body of this book. The first pertains to my style of conceptualization which is psychoanalytically broad-based and eclectic; it freely moves between the early literature, ego psychology, object relations theory, self-psychology, and analytic developmental hypotheses of varying persuasions. Avoiding doctrinaire commitment to any particular model, I strive for integration. The second pertains to the literary realm. While the book rests upon scientific foundations, it does not lack the human touch of poetry. 'Love', 'heart', 'soul', 'anguish', 'despair', 'the weeping child within', and 'desperate self-soothing' are the building blocks of my language to an extent that is comparable to my use of the customary psychoanalytic terminology. A humanizing concomitant of this is that all patients reported here (though amply disguised for the purposes of confidentiality) have been given full names; thus the reader will meet people like Alex Bartlett, Gina Spencer, Sarah Green, and the like, instead of the customary Mr. B., Ms. S., and Ms. G. and so on. The third tendency involves the fact of the book being fundamentally and unabashedly practical. While theoretical grounding does serve as a preamble for delineation of its technical strategies, the book is replete with clinical vignettes and explicatory comments that illustrate the interventions I am proposing as useful. The final tendency involves the fact that the book is not intended to break fresh ground in any sort of dramatic manner; it is aimed to introduce the younger generation of therapists to ways of thinking and working that I, and many others like me, have found clinically useful. I have written it in the hope that some patients of the younger colleagues and students who read it might end up receiving better care as a result. My fervent scribbling is nothing but a therapeutic intervention, even though made indirectly and through the changed attention and voice of other therapists towards their patients. Its goal is to help others help still others better.

1. Initial Assessment

Believe me, every heart has its secret sorrows, which the world knows not; and oftentimes we call a man cold when he is only sad.

Henry Wadsworth Longfellow (1807-1882)

Most psychodynamic psychotherapy cases stumble, come to an impasse, or fail because the patient's suitability and motivation for treatment had not been properly evaluated. Indeed, some psychotherapists take pride in starting a case 'cold' i.e. without a formal assessment of patients' psychopathology, ego-capacities, and psychological-mindedness. This approach, popular with some 'classical' psychoanalysts and those who naively imitate them, often leads to unpleasant surprises. Even in the absence of major fiascos, the lack of agreement between the patient and therapist about the modality and aims of treatment can contribute to future difficulties.

It therefore seems preferable to conduct a proper assessment before deciding upon the start of psychotherapy. This period, starting from the very first moment of contact between the patient and therapist usually spans over one to three sessions, preferably conducted on consecutive days.[1] It provides an opportunity for the assessment of the nature and severity of the patient's psychopathology. It also gives the two parties a chance to get an emotional 'feel' for each other. Through direct questioning, encouragement to elaborate on what has hitherto remained emotionally abbreviated, and patiently listening in a non-judgmental way, the therapist gathers

13

important information about the patient. Through expressing his distress, following the clarifying leads of the therapist's interjections, and listening to his own self, the patient begins to feel more organized. Experiencing a dignified sense of human affinity and feeling 'held' (Winnicott, 1960) in an informed setting, the patient senses an opportunity for betterment and psychic growth.

These developments, while happening silently, are both the result of a proper initial evaluation and the facilitators of it. Their end-point is the mutual agreement between the two parties to undertake the work of psychodynamic psychotherapy with a well-laid out framework and clearly understood plans. However, before arriving at such closure, a number of steps have to be traversed. Some of these steps are concrete and formal, others nearly imperceptible.

Responding To The First Phone Call

The first contact between the therapist and a prospective patient often occurs via telephone. Many things can be learned and many trends can be discerned during this contact. Careful attention should therefore be paid to what the patient says at this time. Both the form and the content of his or her message should be noted. One might find that the patient is cryptic and reluctant to give information. Or, one might note that the patient is talkative and has difficulty restraining himself. To be sure, no definite conclusion can be drawn from these bits and pieces of information but one should tuck them into the back of one's mind and use them as background or as topics of specific investigation once the patient arrives for the first interview. The following clinical encounter illustrates this point.[2]

Clinical Vignette 1

While setting up an appointment via telephone, John Schmidt asked me twice whether my office building had a name, such as the Pan Am Building, the Chrysler Building, and so on. I was intrigued by his insistence, since I had already given him the street number of my building. I also noted that both the buildings he mentioned were in New York and not in Philadelphia, where I practice. I politely repeated that my building did not have a name, keeping my sense of curiosity for later.

During the evaluation session, the first thing I learned was that his full name was John Schmidt, Jr. Next, I gathered that he had a pattern undermining his achievements, in the realm of both romance and business, just when success was around the corner. Much unconscious guilt seemed to lurk in his psyche. To look for the sources of such guilt, I turned to exploring his childhood development. Now I learned that despite having an older brother, it was he who was named after his father. Upon my inquiring about it, he agreed that this was not customary but said that he had never thought about the reasons for this unusual situation. Further questioning revealed that his older brother was mildly retarded. At this point, I ventured a hypothesis. Could it be that his older brother had at first been named after their father, only to be given a different name after the discovery of his retardation? The patient was moved by this suggestion and, though he did not remember hearing any such thing while growing up, began talking about his sadness about his brother and his guilt over his own success, which he had impressively undermined on many occasions.

As all this came pouring out, I became aware that he had unconsciously given me a clue to his problem by insisting on the phone that my building (me) have a bigger, better name than merely a number. Now I brought up our telephone conversation and pointing out that his insistence upon my building (i.e. I) having a better name was a disguised way of 'returning' his borrowed name to his older brother. In essence, it was his way to repair the damage he had felt he had done. The patient began to sob and it was clear that he felt understood in a way that he had never experienced before.

What this dramatic example demonstrates is that by paying close attention to the patient's phone call, one can pick up important clues regarding his or her problem. These can be used to clarify and document the hypotheses that one begins to develop during the evaluative sessions.

In addition to this, there are other guidelines to keep in mind while responding to a call by a prospective patient.

- It is advisable not to hurry in returning the phone call from a person whose name one does not recognize and who might be a prospective patient. Contrary to ordinary 'good manners', it is better that one waits a little (say, from a few hours to even a full day) before answering such a call. An interval of this sort allows one to 'suddenly recall' that one actually knows this person (e.g. he may be an ongoing patient's boyfriend) and should actually not call him or her back. Or, one might receive collateral information (e.g. from another person's phone call) which affects the manner in which one would handle this call.

- It is also good to return a phone call from a potential patient when one can spare some 5-10 minutes of peaceful and uninterrupted time. While lengthy conversation at this point is hardly indicated, having the cushion of a few minutes comes in handy if unexpected complications begin to arise.

- Rather than giving a specific time that is convenient for oneself, the therapist should try to involve the patient in choosing the time for the first appointment. Asking such questions as 'How urgent do you think the situation is?' or 'When was it that you were planning to see me?' permits the patient to negotiate a realistically needed and feasible appointment. More importantly, allowing the patient to exercise some control subtly emphasizes the mutuality of the therapeutic undertaking and helps restore the patient's self-respect at a time of difficulty and self-doubt.

- Patients' questions about fees and billing should be answered in a factual manner. It is inappropriate and misleading to tell a patient to come in saying 'we will discuss the fee issue when you are here'. This can put the patient, who comes and reveals his inner turmoil, in a disadvantage if he can not afford the therapist's fees and has to be referred elsewhere.

- Conditions put by the patient for coming or not coming should neither be accepted nor rejected. One should emphasize that both parties need to have open-mindedness about such matters. Neither undue flexibility nor stern rigidity is helpful. What is needed is a firm adherence to the stance of neutrality, curiosity, and respect for the complexity of mental processes.

- It is considerate to inform the patient right away of any constraints from one's own side. For instance, if one does not have time to take a new patient or one is leaving soon for a long vacation, the patient should be informed of it. Such forthrightness helps preclude feelings of betrayal and may prevent even more serious complications in highly regressed and needy patients.

- One should give clear and specific directions about the location of one's office and not assume that the patient knows his way around. Often, the patient's lateness for his first appointment is the result of the vague directions given by the therapist rather than of resistance and enactment.

THE PATIENT'S ARRIVAL FOR THE INITIAL INTERVIEW

The patient's appearance, behavior, and manner of arrival also can provide significant information even before a formal evaluation has begun. There are many things to be noted here: is the patient appropriately dressed? How is his personal hygiene? Are there any outstanding mannerisms, scars, or tattoos? Does he look angry, sad, happy, nervous? Also, does he come on time? Does he arrive late or, conversely, too early? Or does the patient come at a completely different time than was agreed upon?

CLINICAL VIGNETTE 2

After having waited for Gina Spencer, who had sought a consultation with me, for about twenty minutes, I received a frantic phone call from her. She was looking for my office in a building five blocks away. Where did I say my office was? When I repeated my address, she realized her 'mistake' and wanted to know if she could still come over for her appointment. Thinking that not much time would be left by the time she arrived, I offered her an appointment on a subsequent day. She apologized for her 'mistake' and accepted my offer.

On the day before Gina's second appointment, I came out of my office after the last patient of the day had left to find her sitting in my waiting room. She was enraged and said that she felt very humiliated by my having 'abused' her in this fashion! Puzzled, I asked what it was that she felt I had done to her. She responded by saying that I had kept her waiting for an entire hour while seeing another patient. It took her a few minutes to realize that she had come a day earlier than her scheduled appointment!

Now, there were these two enactments even before we began a formal consultation. First, she went to the wrong building and was frantically looking for me. Second, she came at the wrong time and felt 'abused' by me. I kept these in mind and decided to see what in our 'third' encounter (i.e. our first formal interview) might shed light on the communications contained in these enactments. (Besides, of course, I noted the propensity toward acting out, resistance, sado-masochism, and use of paranoid defenses).

In her subsequent appointment, for which she arrived punctually, Gina told me that her main difficulty was constant anger at men, sexual disinterest, and depressive mood swings with occasional suicidal thoughts. She revealed that her father, to whom she was very attached, had abruptly left the family when she was five years old. She never saw him afterwards and was always 'searching' for him. When she was eight years old, her mother remarried. Her stepfather sexually abused her until she was thirteen years old. At this time, the patient moved out the house and started living with an aunt. As this material came out, I brought to her attention that her frantically 'searching' for me the first time and feeling 'abused' by me the second time were perhaps her ways of putting me in the place of her real father and stepfather, respectively. Till the time I was in either position, I added, she could not relate to me. Perhaps she needed a third chance, a new experience. The patient began to cry and, after composing herself, revealed more details of her anguished life.

The point I am trying to make here is that enactments as gross as these cannot be ignored. They must be thought about and recognized as up for discussion. Vigilance combined with tact is the key here. This applies not only to the patient's appearance and behavior but also to the things that they might bring along with them.

CLINICAL VIGNETTE 3

As Alex Bartlett, a thirty-four year-old lawyer, entered my office for his first interview, I noticed that he was carrying a popular magazine in his hand. Sitting down, he put the magazine on the table near him. The session proceeded along conventional lines while, in a corner of my mind, I kept wondering about the magazine. Oblivious to my concern, he went on to describe the interpersonal difficulties that had led to his seeking help. He said while finding women was not difficult for him, keeping them involved certainly seemed a problem. One after another, they left him complaining of his aloofness and self-sufficiency. I found myself looking at the magazine he had brought along but decided to wait before saying anything about it.

Moving on to his family background, Alex revealed that his parents had divorced when he was four and, for the following three years, his mother toiled hard to raise him and his two older sisters. She worked long hours and expected the children to be well-behaved. Alex grew up to be a courteous young man who was repeatedly abandoned by women who found him nice but unengaging. He suffered greatly since he wanted involvement and mutuality in his life. At this point, I asked him about the magazine. He seemed surprised and said that he had brought it for reading in the waiting room. I asked him if he thought that I would have no reading material there and if he could see how this seemingly innocuous behavior betrayed his anxiety about dependence and attachment. I added that perhaps it was this sort of 'self-sufficiency' that was found unacceptable (and unconsciously rejecting) by his girlfriends. He was taken aback but could readily see the dynamics in action. His eyes filled up with tears and he said, 'But I can't help it. I have always relied upon myself.' Yet there was a clear sense in the office that an aspect of his problematic 'character armor' (Reich, 1933) had already been made ego-dystonic.

I can offer many other examples of this sort but will suffice to say that the therapist must note and make use of the messages contained in the physical possessions patients bring with them.

There are still other things to observe. For instance, the arrival of an adult patient (who is not psychotic, organically impaired, or a fresh immigrant to the country) in the company of a relative or friend should raise questions in the consultant's mind. Is there ego impairment here? Paranoia? Separation anxiety? Some phobia? Enactment of some unconscious fantasy? Such behavior could reflect any of these or might imply something completely different. The point is to observe it, consider it data. Similarly, the observation that the patient arrives carrying too many things should be silently registered. It may lead to something or it may not, but it cannot be ignored. Finally, our own very first feelings about the patient should be jotted down in the back of our minds for further private exploration. This might yield useful information about either or both parties in the dyad of a consultation.

Assessing The Need For Treatment

Nature And Severity Of Symptoms

The first formal step in initial assessment consists of a relatively straightforward exploration of the patient's presenting symptoms. Such inquiry might begin with a simple statement like: 'What seems to be the reason that has led you to come here?' or, even more briefly: 'Tell me what brings you here?' This would lead the patient to describe his or her predominant difficulties. The interviewer, after listening patiently for a while should summarize for the patient the main symptoms and, in doing so, organize the relevant clusters of complaints. For instance, the interviewer might say: 'From what you have told me so far, it seems that you are experiencing three main difficulties: first, depression, including crying spells, hopelessness, and occasional suicidal thoughts; second, an increasing alienation from your family involving disagreements about your boyfriend and your place of residence; and third, some confusion about whether you wish to continue your education or drop out from school altogether'. Such an intervention helps the patient organize his or her thinking, demonstrates to the patient that the therapist has already begun his work, and, by providing identifiable categories to the often diffuse distress, gives the patient an intellectual handle on it. It might limit the patient's freedom somewhat, but this can be rectified by asking open-ended questions pertaining to what one might have missed somewhat later in the interview.

Once the patient's main symptoms are identified, more detailed investigation of each should follow. The account now provided by the patient might be fleshed out further by the interviewer's asking more direct questions, preventing the patient from becoming too tangential, and exploring the presence or absence of secondary and related symptoms. In the case of depression, for instance, these might include excessive drinking, incapacity for caring for children, and manic episodes. As the details of each cluster of symptoms become clear, the interviewer might begin thinking about the possible connections between the various clusters. However, it is preferable to keep such early hypotheses to oneself at this point.

While remaining reserved on this front, the therapist should by no means stay passive and non-directive. He should allow the patient to elaborate and offer details but he should also feel free to stop the patient from going on and on about what has already been established. More importantly, he should not shy away from what appears difficult and anxiety-producing to the patient. In this context, the following reminder by Gill and Redlich (1954) is important.

The technique of quickly leaving painful subjects often is interpreted by the patient as a reluctance to attack major difficulties. A patient's anxiety may even be heightened by the feeling that if the therapist is fearful, the problem must be serious indeed. A bold attack which shows that the therapist knows what he is about, that he can lay his finger on the trouble and is not afraid, may not only be very reassuring but may go far toward helping the patient overcome the ever-present tendencies to evasion, whether these are conscious or not. (p. 31)

One area of pain and anxiety to which an entire section of this book (Chapter Five) is devoted pertains to suicide, which must be directly and fearlessly explored, especially when the patient's presenting complaints involve depression. Similar forthrightness needs to be maintained vis-à-vis addictions and sexual deviations. The calm, unhurried but firm manner of the therapist lays the groundwork for the 'working alliance' (Greenson, 1965) within the dyad.

Level Of Character Organization

Assuming that the patient is non-psychotic (since the presence of psychosis aborts a dynamic interview and reverts it back to the traditional psychiatric history-taking[3]), the essential task of this part of evaluation is to distinguish between neurotic and borderline levels of personality organization. Using the terms 'oedipal' and 'pre-oedipal' for these two groups respectively, Greenspan (1977) has outlined seven dimensions of personality functioning that help differentiate between them:[4]

(i) capacity for distinguishing internal versus external reality; (ii) cohesion, organization and resistance to fragmentation even under stress of the self and object representations; (iii) capacity for experiencing and perceiving a variety of discriminated affect states; (iv) level of defenses,(v) capacity to modulate impulses appropriate to external situation; (vi) capacity for gen-

uine attachment and separation, and for the experience of sadness and mourning; and (vii) capacity for
integration of love and hate. (p. 385)

Within the interview situation, coming to grips with the above
largely translates into the exploration of the following three areas.

(1) *The degree of identity consolidation.* In the neurotic character
organization, there is a well-established identity while in the borderline organization there is identity diffusion (Kernberg, 1975,
1984; Akhtar, 1984, 1992a). The features of identity diffusion include markedly contradictory character traits, temporal discontinuity in the self-experience, feelings of emptiness, gender dysphoria, subtle body-image disturbances, and inordinate ethnic and
moral relativism (Akhtar, 1984). Not all of these features can be
elicited and explored to an equal degree through formal questioning. Some (e.g. feelings of emptiness) are more evident in the patient's complaints, while others (e.g. temporal discontinuity in the
self-experience) become clear only through obtaining a step-by-
step longitudinal account of the patient's life. Still other features
(e.g. subtle disturbances of gender identity) are discernible, at least
in the beginning mainly through the overall manner of the patien-
t's relating to the interviewer. Yet it is helpful to ask the patient to
describe himself. One might say something like this: 'Now that you
have told me about your difficulties, can you please describe yourself as a person?' In the description offered by the patient, one
should look for consistency versus contradiction, clarity versus
confusion, solidity versus emptiness, a well developed sense of
masculinity or femininity versus gender dysphoria, and a sense of
ethnicity and inner morality versus the lack of any historical or
communal anchor.

If the patient is unable to provide a coherent description, this
should not be immediately construed as implying identity diffusion. This could be due to anxiety, lack of psychological mindedness, cultural factors, poor verbal skills or low intelligence. These
factors should be ruled out before making a conclusion regarding
the presence or absence of identity diffusion in a given instance.

Sensing difficulty in the communicative path of the patient, the
therapist might decide to help him by conducting the inquiry in a
piecemeal fashion. For instance, he might ask about the patient's

religious beliefs, practices, and their continuity with what was handed down to him during childhood; feelings of ethnicity and of belonging to a certain regional or communal group; continuity of contact with friends and associates from earlier periods of life; clarity and stability of vocational goals; sublimations and hobbies; and so on. He may then surmise the status of the patient's identity based on the information gathered. A patient might not be able to describe himself well, yet may turn out to posses a consolidated identity. Conversely, one might come across in a patient

> peripheral areas of self-experience that are contradictory to a well-integrated, central area of subjective experience, peripheral areas that the patient experiences as ego-alien or ego-dystonic, not fitting into his otherwise integrated picture of himself. These isolated areas may be an important source of intrapsychic conflict or interpersonal difficulties but should not be equated with identity diffusion. (Kernberg, 1984, p. 37)

(2) *The nature of predominant ego defenses.* The 'neurotic' or higher level character organization is characterized by the predominance of repression as the main ego defense and the borderline organization by the predominance of splitting and related defenses (Kernberg, 1967, 1975, 1984; Volkan, 1976). Splitting manifests in five different ways (Akhtar and Byrne, 1983): (i) inability to tolerate much ambivalence, (ii) intensification of affects, (iii) reckless decision-making process, (iv) ego-syntonic impulsivity, and (v) marked oscillations of self-esteem. The individual using splitting tends to have an all-or-nothing approach to life. He sees good and bad as mutually exclusive. He is overly controlled or loses all control. He attacks the entire problem and gets overwhelmed or avoids the problem altogether and feels defeated. He has a tendency towards 'now or never; murderous rage or total denial of anger; either my way or your way; either this way or not at all' (Schulz, 1980, p. 184).

In the interview situation, the patient's verbal productions, as well as his overall attitudes, give hints toward the existence, or more accurately, the predominance, of splitting. Confronting the patient with contradictions in the information provided by him and seeing his response also helps discern the tendency toward splitting. It may help distinguish borderline from potentially psychotic levels of organization (Kernberg, 1984). Demonstrating gross psychic contradictions (e.g. a Catholic nun moonlighting as a stripper, a tongue-tied and shy individual being a stunning public orator) to the patient leads in the former instance to anxiety and awkwardness coupled with recognition of contradictions and a temporarily improved observing ego. In the latter, however, such confrontation leads to a greater tenacity of compartmentalizations and recourse to increasingly odd 'logic' to defend the validity of keeping ill-fitting sectors of personality apart.

(3) *The nature of object relations.* Taking a detailed family history (including questions about parents and their marriage, siblings, and, if the patient is married, their spouse) provides an opportunity to asses the patient's capacity for meaningful object relations. The patient who has a higher level of character organization (e.g. obsessional, phobic, hysterical) shows the capacity for relating to others as truly separate individuals with their own strengths, weaknesses, and independent motivations. The one with a lower level character organization (1) gives premium to his own feelings (e.g. 'I hate him', 'I find him adorable') over the actual description of someone else (e.g. 'My mother is a school teacher and a very kind person'), (2) uses extreme adjectives (e.g. 'She is brilliant!'), (3) fails to take into account the concerns and motivations others may have independently of him, and (4) has few non-exploitative relationships (as evidenced by lack of concern for nephews, nieces, and pets, i.e. from whom one can derive little direct benefit). When these features are prominent, the character organization is usually in the borderline range even though phenotypically the patient might appear to be functioning better. A marked presence of the fourth element is suggestive of antisocial personality disorder.

ASSESSING SUITABILITY FOR TREATMENT

Psychological Mindedness

A quick survey of the literature reveals that different people mean different things by 'psychological mindedness' or at least emphasize different aspects. Reiser (1971), for instance, delineated three components of psychological-mindedness: (1) sensitivity to symbolic meanings and to situational resemblances between life events in historical context, (2) empathy for others' affective experiences, and (3) interest in human behavior and the motives that underlie it. He emphasized that psychological-mindedness, in contrast to curiosity, is inwardly directed. It is more passive, reflective, and receptive than curiosity, which is driving and compelling. Lower et al. (1972) described psychological-mindedness as including 'a capacity for insight, introspective, intuition, verbality, remembering dreams and fantasies, awareness of transference, of internal conflict; sensitivity to own feelings and curiosity about drives' (p. 615). Applebaum (1973) proposed the following definition: 'A person's ability to see relationships among thoughts, feelings, and actions, with the goal of learning the meanings and causes of his experience and behavior' (p. 36). He distinguished such psychological interest for purposes of understanding oneself and others from the intellectualized, exhibitionistic, merely playful, or self-condemnatory uses of introspection.

While these investigators do offer many 'clinical pearls', it is Coltart (1988) who provided the most detailed guidelines about the assessment of psychological-mindedness in the diagnostic interview. Though acknowledging that the whole is often greater than the sum of its parts, she outlined nine points 'in an approximate order of discovery, rather than importance, under two headings' (p. 819): the history, and developments in the interview arising from the history. Under the first heading, Coltart suggested that the diagnostician should look for:

> 1. The capacity to give a history which deepens, acquires more coherence, and becomes textually more substantial as it goes on... 2. The capacity to give such a history without much prompting, and a history which gives the listener an increasing awareness that the patient feels currently related in himself, to his own story; properly—if unhappily—the product of the connective aetiology of his life's circumstances... 3. The capacity to bring up memories with appropriate affects. (p. 819)

Under the second heading, Coltart included the following:

> 4. Some awareness in the patient that he has an un-
> conscious mental life... 5. Some capacity to step back,
> if only momentarily, from self-experience, and to ob-
> serve it reflectively—either spontaneously, or with the
> help of a simple interpretation from the assessor, who
> should make opportunity for this sort of
> intervention... 6. A capacity, or more strongly a wish,
> to accept and handle increased responsibility for the
> self... 7. Imagination... 8. Some capacity for achieve-
> ment, and some realistic self-esteem... 9. Overall im-
> pression... something deeply recognizable, but ulti-
> mately not fully definable, about the assessor's experi-
> ence of a thorough, intense, working consultation
> with a psychologically minded person. (pp. 819-820)

I am in agreement with Coltart. However, I think that she became a bit over-inclusive in listing capacity for achievement under
psychological-mindedness. On the other hand, she did not include
some other ways to assess the patient's psychological-mindedness.
For instance, a patient who has kept an ongoing journal displays a
capacity for reflectiveness, a wish for psychic dialogue, and a respect for mental life. The same applies to a patient who spontaneously offers a dream during the initial evaluation. This is especially significant if the patient is not in the mental health field and
thus not biased in that direction. Yet another evidence of psychological-mindedness is the patient's spontaneous offering of a ge-
netic explanation of either his or her own or someone else's behavior.

To summarize, it seems that psychological-mindedness is best
reflected by observing the following things: (1) *a capacity for reflective self-observation* as evidenced by the patient's giving a coherent
and affectively resonant history as well as by his or her ability to be
aware (or become aware during the interview) of internal conflicts;
(2) *an interest in one's mental life* as evidenced by a history of having
kept journals, and by spontaneously mentioning dreams and fantasies in the initial interview; (3) *a belief in psychic causality* as evidenced by the patient's offering a genetic explanation of his or her

own or another's behavior and by his or her capacity to entertain a mental basis for certain accidents, onset of a physical illness, and so on; and (4) *a readiness to see symbolic meanings* and enter into a metaphorical dialogue as evidenced by a positive, even welcoming, response to a trial interpretation.[5]

Two caveats are in order here. First, the presence of only one among these four factors should not lead to the conclusion that the patient is psychologically-minded. Two, an attempt should be made to distinguish an actual deficiency in psychological-mindedness from its pallor due to anxiety in the interview situation. Supportive, empathic remarks may diminish the anxiety and improve psychological mindedness in the latter but not in the former instance.

Other Mental Functions

(1) *Benign regression.* In order to enter and benefit from dynamic psychotherapy, an individual must posses the capacity to renounce logic and reality on a transient and ego-replenishing basis. Without such 'benign regression' (Balint, 1959, 1968), psychotherapy tends to become a mere intellectual exercise. The way to assess this capacity is ask the patient about their leisure time (e.g. Sundays, vacations), their being able to have peaceful solitude, and their ability to play with children and pets.[6]

(2) *Ego strength.* Since dynamic psychotherapy can stir up latent conflicts and cause anxiety, it is important to have some sense of the patient's ego strength. This can be ascertained by asking the patient how he deals with stressful situations (e.g. examinations, job interviews, children's illness) as well as by observing how the patient conducts himself in the interview himself. Incapacity to tolerate anxiety and poor impulse control are suggestive of a weak ego and, therefore, negative prognostic indicators in-depth psychotherapy.

(3) *The 'intermediate area of experience'.* According to Winnicott (1953), the 'intermediate area of experience' refers to the psychic space where a confluence of reality and unreality occurs even though such matters do not form its content per se. It is where imagination is born and paradox reigns supreme. It contains phenomena that are subjectively experienced and are neither questioned nor not questioned for their literal verity. Its clinical impor-

tance lies in the fact that transference phenomena should stay within this area and not become too 'real' in order to be interpretable. Assessment of the patient's capacity in this regard can be done by questions pertaining to the patient's ability to play, create, and enjoy fiction, movies and poetry, all of which require a make-believe sort of mental attitude. His responses to the therapist's tentative interpretations which offer imaginative ways of understanding his problems is also telling in this regard.

(4) *Superego*. Some assessment of superego functioning is also essential. A harsh superego makes the patient feel unworthy of deep and sustained help and prepares the ground for a 'negative therapeutic reaction' (Freud, 1923) once the treatment gets underway. Resistance to uncovering deeper layers of psyche where anxiety, guilt, and shame-producing wishes and fantasies lurk can be strengthened by a strict superego. Too lax a superego can also pose problems, with the patient lying, withholding information, and misrepresenting financial resources in order to pay a lower than realistic fee for treatment.

ASSESSING FEASIBILITY OF TREATMENT

While the assessment of psychopathology yields information about the need for treatment and the assessment of psychological mindedness, ego strength, and superego function yields information about the suitability for treatment, it is the assessment of the patients motivation and his or her reality situation that reveals whether a meaningful treatment can actually be established.

Motivation

Patients who are themselves desirous of change are the ones most suited for in-depth psychotherapy. Recognizing, at least to some extent, their own role in the subjective and interpersonal distress they are feeling, such individuals are better prepared to take a look at their own selves with the psychic lens created in the therapeutic dyad. It should however be acknowledged, in all fairness, that most patients arriving at the psychotherapist's door are not so prepared; they seek symptomatic relief. Here the assessment of self-concern as well as the concern the patient shows towards others who are impacted by his 'symptoms' is important. Finally, there are patients who seek treatment largely at the behest of an exhausted spouse, irate parent, or disgruntled employer. The temptation to regard these patients as lacking motivation is great. However, simply because the patient has been 'forced' to come by someone else does not automatically translate into lack of desire for change. Careful evaluation of each individual case in point is therefore indicated though with the following caveats in mind.

First, it should be remembered that motivation does not refer to conscious motivation alone. Klauber (1981) has eloquently made this point:

> What commonly brings the patient is the pressure of his immediate suffering, usually on himself, but not infrequently on his doctor or his family. But in any case, his conscious motivation whether for analysis or against it, is only a partial indicator of his unconscious motivation. It is his unconscious motivation which has to be determined—the repressed wish, so to speak, behind the manifest content of his presentation and the relevance of this wish to the present crisis in his life. (p. 151)

Second, those individuals who seem very well-motivated for change sometimes turn out not to be so; a nucleus of hard resistance at times dwells deep within their psyche. Patients who have extensively read psychiatric and psychoanalytic literature and seem gifted in their grasp of unconscious trends at times turn out to be operating largely from a false self constellation (Balsam, 1984). Others, while appearing quite devoted to the therapeutic enterprise reveal tenacious 'some day...' fantasies of an entirely conflict-free existence that keep them from being truly involved in a process of psychic change (Akhtar, 1996). Sadly, these resistances are not infrequent among those working in the mental health field.

Third, those who claim to have been pushed to seek treatment by others might have unconsciously engineered such referral by incremental doses of unacceptable behavior. The help-seeking cry of others on their behalf reflects the repudiated healthy parts of their own personality; these have been deposited into others by 'healthy projective identification' (Hamilton, 1986). The following observation by Armstrong (2000) pointedly underscores this dynamic.

The man sent by his spouse or the woman sent by her sister must have felt some inkling of pain, some unconscious connection with the relative's complaint to seek the treatment. It will be the therapist's task, one more difficult than with the person who is self-motivated, to locate that pain. (p. 161)

Finally, while motivation is an attribute that the patient brings with himself, it can also be 'co-created' during the clinical encounter. The therapist's grasp of the patient's inner reality can, at times, mobilize the patient in new and powerful ways.

CLINICAL VIGNETTE 4

Norman Liebowitz, a thirty-two year-old internist from a regional medical center, came to see me for 'depression'. From all external appearances, he seemed successful: he was young, handsome, financially stable, and physically healthy. He was also happily married and recently had become a father. It was this last epoch that I felt had, paradoxically, triggered the depression he was feeling. Support to this line of thinking was given by the account of prior masochistic mishaps associated with his graduation from college and from medical school.

As the interview proceeded, Dr. Liebowitz abruptly stopped and said while all he had said so far was true, there was something else that was troubling him even more. This 'something' had been with him for many years but he had never been able to talk about it with anyone. I responded by gently encouraging him to say more about what this hidden problem was and also about the concerns that had led him to keep it a secret. After some hesitation, Dr. Liebowitz revealed that he liked to chew upon cats' nails. He would frequent the houses of friends and acquaintances and, at times, scout the neighborhood to find a cat. Holding the animal up in his arms, he would bite off a chip from its nails. He kept these bits and pieces in a glass vial and chewed upon them at his leisure. As the interview progressed, a second interaction with cats emerged. He liked to bring a cat's face very, very close to his own face and then breathe in the air that came out of the cat's nostrils. Both these acts gave him deep gratification though he also worried about their apparent oddity and did not quite know what to make of them.

The next day, while describing his family background, Dr. Liebowitz came upon the topic of his mother. He sighed, saying: 'You don't want to know about her. She is so controlling and so intrusive that I cannot describe. She lives about a thousand miles from here but I constantly feel her claws digging in to me.' As he said this, he grabbed the upper part of his left arm with his right hand, making the latter appear like a claw, and dug his nails into the skin. Seeing the connection between the biting off of a cat's nails and the alleged claw of his mother on his arm, I said: 'Did you notice what you just said?' He was puzzled. 'What?' he responded. I said, 'What do you make of you using the word "claws" in connection with your mother and how do you connect her "claws" with a cat's nails?' He was dumbfounded but gradually became somber and began to talk about his chronic difficulty of maintaining an optimal distance from his mother. With further elaboration during the session, the biting off of the cat's nails and breathing the air coming out of the cat's nostrils could be seen to symbolize the two sides of this distance-closeness conflict. As this clarification settled in our dialogue, I could see him become more animated and curious about his intrapsychic life.

In the end, it seems that the issue of motivation is far from simple. The categorical division of 'motivated' or 'unmotivated' patients should therefore be put aside in favor of the following dimensional queries. What aspect of his psychopathology is the patient motivated to get help for? What has caused this motivation? What is his conscious motivation and what is his unconscious motivation? How can one mobilize forces within the patient to enhance his motivation for psychic growth? What fears, concerns, and self-defeating tendencies might be responsible for his low motivation? To what extent, these can be brought to the patient's awareness and with what beneficial result? And so on. It is this kind of a broad-based and thoughtful approach to the issue of the patient's motivation that yields more productive information.

Reality Factors

The psychotherapeutic enterprise, despite its imaginary and imaginative dimensions, must be firmly anchored in reality. This is not only true vis-à-vis the therapeutic framework and the interpersonal boundaries it is dependent upon (see Chapter Two for more details) but also applies to the very fact of taking a patient into treatment. In other words, certain realistic conditions must be met before one agrees to treat a patient in intensive psychotherapy. Some certainty of sustained financial resources, for instance, is necessary. Without a proper investigation of this, the treatment at times comes to a screeching halt and, because a psychodynamic process involving transference and countertransference has been set into motion by this time, it becomes very difficult to sort out the role of the reality impediment in the continuation of care. (See Chapter Three for more details on the role of money in psychotherapy.)

Another requirement is that the patient resides within a reasonable distance of the therapist's office. A patient who lives far away might make earnest promises to maintain regular attendance for the sessions but generally fails to do so once the difficulty of travel meets the inevitable resistance to psychological uncovering. Therapists who are financially or otherwise needy are as vulnerable to compromises of judgment in such situations as are the renowned and charismatic 'specialists' sought out by long distance patients.

While by and large it is inadvisable to take patients who live a long distance away from the therapist's office, there might be exceptions to this rule. Three such situations are: (i) the distance is rendered manageable by rapid means of transport, (ii) there is no adequately trained psychotherapist in the patient's vicinity, (iii) the patient is a mental health professional for whom the treatment is a part of psychoanalytic training and there is no training analyst where the patient lives or works. To be sure, problematic scenarios can lurk in the background of these situations as well but they do require a more sympathetic consideration than where the pressure to be treated by a particular, usually renowned, therapist is mostly based on the idealization of him.

In these latter circumstances, the capacity of the therapist to contain and manage the prospective patient's idealization becomes crucial. A highly nuanced approach is needed in dealing with those who call after reading a book one has authored or after hearing a lecture one delivered somewhere out of town. This approach must avoid the extremes of defensive recoil and refusing to see the patient altogether or getting seduced into starting a treatment under unrealistic circumstances. Rather than rejecting the patient, the therapist might offer a consultation of about two to three hours in length (with or without a short break) with the explicit statement that this would not lead to an on-going treatment. Such consultation should encompass not only the tasks outlined above but also explore the patient's idealization of the therapist with the hope to bring it to a temporary closure; the reasons for it can be understood and resolved in a future treatment under more realistic circumstances.

A different problem is presented by individuals who seek out of town treatment because they themselves are pillars of their society and cannot afford to be 'discovered' seeking help. While exceptions exist, a consistent exploration of their vulnerability to shame can help them overcome this resistance.

CLINICAL VIGNETTE 5

Max Robinson, a sixty year-old wealthy businessman from a small city some one hundred miles away from my office, consulted me in the midst of a marital crisis. His wife had discovered that he was having an extramarital affair and had threatened to divorce him. As matters got more heated, the prior occurrence of two more infidelities came out. Asking for her forgiveness, Max told her that he had been emotionally troubled for a long time and would seek psychiatric help.

The evaluation that followed revealed a history of much greater sexual promiscuity than these three affairs suggested. Max had been restless for years and his sexual escapades had taken place in the setting of chronic boredom. Placed alongside a distinguished work record and overall stability of personality functioning, such contact hunger, coupled with a nearly total inability to love anyone, suggested the possible diagnosis of narcissistic personality disorder. I made a recommendation of psychodynamic psychotherapy on a twice a week basis with the consideration of converting it to psychoanalysis in the future. Clearly, it was not possible for him to undertake this treatment with me since he lived quite far from my office. Fortunately there was a psychoanalyst who practiced in his town; this was someone I knew and respected. The patient, it turned out, was unwilling to see this analyst, claiming he would be profoundly ashamed if someone in town saw him go in and out of a 'shrink's' office. This gave me an opportunity to explore the feelings of inferiority that were hidden inside of him and had, in part, fueled his promiscuity; the idea was that if a woman agreed to sleep with him, he must not be all that bad. As we were able to link his hesitation over going to the local analyst with his chronic self-doubt, Max's opposition to my recommendation diminished.

RECOMMENDING TREATMENT

Once the core information about the patient's psychopathology has been gathered, his suitability for dynamic psychotherapy determined, and a sense of whether such treatment is realistically feasible has been gained, the therapist is in the position of making a recommendation. While there are always exceptions in the clinical situation, the choice, at this point, between recommending psychoanalysis, psychodynamic psychotherapy, or supportive interventions rests upon a telescoping of the three sets of information (psychopathology, ego and superego functions, and motivation and realities) into a composite gestalt. This does not rule out the fact that the patient's symptoms alone can, at times, affect the choice of treatment modality. For instance, three types of symptoms should give one pause while recommending in-depth treatment, be it psychoanalysis proper or psychodynamic psychotherapy. These include (i) symptoms that are bizarre (e.g. communication with extraterrestrial beings); (ii) symptoms that are pleasurable (e.g. excessive drinking, sexual promiscuity in younger narcissistic patients); and (iii) symptoms that stand by themselves and are tenacious (e.g. monosymptomatic hypochondriasis). This last point has been made most emphatically by Klauber (1981) who states that 'the lack of capacity for varied forms of displacement implies a near-delusional mechanism' (p. 155).

All in all, the patients who have a mild to moderate degree of psychopathology, a higher level of character organization, outstanding psychological mindedness, good ego strength, well integrated superego, strong motivation, and relatively easy realities, should be taken into or referred for psychoanalysis proper (Bachrach & Leaff, 1978; Rothstein, 1982; Zimmerman,1982). Those patients who have moderate to severe psychopathology, an overall borderline level of personality organization regardless of its phenotypical picture, high or medium psychological mindedness, some compromise of ego and superego functions, moderately strong motivation, and only somewhat compromised realities, should be regarded as being suitable for psychodynamic psychotherapy. Finally, those who are very severely ill, betray a psychotic level of character organization, have medium or low level of psychological mindedness, moderate to severe impairment of ego and superego functions, weak motivation, and difficult realities, should be treated with supportive interventions including the adjunct measures of medications, group interventions and even hospitalization. However, these guidelines must be treated as such and not turned into rigid rules. Their aim is to underscore the plausibility of differential therapeutics in this realm, not to box in the clinician in prefabricated and inviolable categories.

Once the therapist has arrived at such clarity, he should inform the patient that his diagnostic evaluation is over and share his conclusions with the patient in simple, jargon-free language. He might include in his comments hints of how he arrived at his conclusions. Quoting something the patient had said, recounting a particular emotional outburst, and reminding the patient of a slip of the tongue enhance the patient's sense of participation and mutuality even at this phase. This, in turn, facilitates the patient's receptivity to the information being given.

Two other things should be kept in mind. Firstly, it might be good to preface one's comments with the caveat that conclusions arrived at in one to three sessions are necessarily tentative. The interviewer might also indicate at this time the need for further investigations of a social (i.e. family interview), psychometric, or laboratory kind, if he thinks that these might help to clarify the situation. Secondly, while using ordinary language is preferable there is no reason to be wishy-washy or apologetic if a patient asks for a specific psychiatric diagnosis. Exploring the patient's reasons for asking this might reveal further, significant information. However, such exploration should not be used as a delay tactic, and a patient who wants to know his diagnosis should be told. The emphasis in statements made to the patient must, however, remain upon the patient's subjective experience and not upon the behavioral concomitants typical of the nosological entity though these might have to be included as well. The following ways of explaining borderline and narcissistic personality labels illustrate this point well:

- *Borderline personality disorder.* 'As we grow from a child to an adult, we develop two capacities: one is to want and need "good" things, such as "good" relationships, "good" love, "good" sex, "good" job, "good" house, and so on. The other capacity we develop is to tolerate the disappointing fact that we will not get "good" stuff all the time. The individual who has a borderline personality disorder has the first capacity but lacks the second one. As a result, when faced with disappointments, he gets very hurt and like any other person who is frequently hurt, he gets angry. This anger comes in the way of the mind's peaceful functioning in the realms of both his relationships and vocation. Life gets splintered and is lived in pieces. At times, the individual vents his rage on self and others or tries to get rid of it by numbing his mind (with the use of substances) or distracting himself by impulsive gratifications. All in all, borderline personality disorder is a very painful condition to have.'

- *Narcissistic personality disorder.* 'The person with a narcissistic personality disorder is someone who is preoccupied with his own self. While it might come across as such, this is hardly a matter of vanity. The fact is that the person secretly feels quite worried about his own self and carries a profound vulnerability to shame. Having been raised on praise without much love and affection, such a person has become dependent upon admiration. This is what he constantly seeks. He feels perpetually compelled to improve his talents, polish his image, and "sell" himself to others. Now, all this takes a lot of effort, and energy. It is truly tiresome. Besides it has the painful consequence of his becoming unable to pay attention to others and also not feeling really loved by anybody; he feels that people like him only because of what he has accomplished not for who he is. He feels alone in this world. While socially successful and admired by others, the narcissistic person lives in a private world of self-doubt, inferiority and insatiable longing for genuine love and acceptance.'

This manner of telling the patient's diagnosis to him should put to rest the prevalent notion that patients misunderstand diagnostic terminology and are narcissistically injured by it. In holding onto this old-fashioned idea, one is liable to overlook that the interviewer's cryptic attitude, fudging, and uncomfortable avoidance can also have alienating and adverse effects on the patient.

Following the discussion of the nature of the patient's problem, the focus should shift to issues of its treatment. The interviewer should now inform the patient of what he thinks is the ideal treatment for the patient's malady, explaining, especially if asked, the reasons for this recommendation. The patient should also be informed, especially if things are unclear, of alternate approaches to treating the condition involved, and encouraged to ask questions about anything that seems unclear Questions raised by the patient should be answered factually, and the interviewer should not derail or mystify the patient by 'interpreting' the reasons behind such questions. For instance, the patient may ask why the frequency of two to three times a week is needed for dynamic psychotherapy. Or, he might ask about the difference between psychoanalysis and psychotherapy. Subtle controversies in the field notwithstanding, it is possible to answer such questions in a simple, straightforward way. Regarding frequency, one might say the following: 'the problems we are dealing with here are deep and solving them requires the sort of access to your inner world that can only be provided by such frequency.' One might explain the difference between psychoanalysis and psychotherapy not only in terms of frequency of visits and the use of couch but, to a certain extent, in terms of the nature of the patient's activity (i.e., free association) and the therapist's 'quieter' stance vis-à-vis the patient's report of his thoughts, feelings, fantasies, and dreams. In the end, it is the therapist's straightforward and collaborative manner in dealing with the patient's questions that counts.

CONCLUDING REMARKS

In this chapter, I have attempted to offer an account of what constitutes a thorough initial assessment of a potential patient for psychodynamic psychotherapy. I have divided my comments into the categories of (i) forming early impressions, (ii) assessing psychopathology, (iii) assessing psychological mindedness and other ego functions, and (iv) assessing the patient's motivation and realities that might impact upon the feasibility of proper treatment.[7] I have described how pooling the four sets of data helps choose a treatment modality and then described the process of making recommendations to the patient, answering his questions, and, through all this, beginning to set the ground rules for treatment being undertaken.

Conducting these tasks is hardly restricted to gathering objective information; the therapist's subjective experience plays a key role throughout the evaluation process. Indeed, vigilance towards early 'countertransference' yields all sorts of useful clinical data, as I have already shown in this chapter. What I wish to underscore now is that while the arousal of strong feelings in the therapist does not necessarily preclude his taking the patient into on-going treatment, circumstances where this might be the case do exist. Intense discomfort with a patient based upon cultural differences and/or the nature of psychopathology at hand might, at times, not be 'containable' by the therapist's work ego. Instead of becoming unduly valiant, it might then be preferable not to take the patient into treatment. Politics, the last taboo in the clinical field, can also contribute to insurmountable difficulties. Finally, there is the issue of the therapist's competence to treat a particular patient. While all sorts of professional and legal checks and balances exist in order to assure this, ultimately the assessment of one's competence rests upon a honest self-scrutiny and fearless soul searching.[8]

This brings up the fact that in-depth psychotherapy constitutes an intrapsychic and interpersonal journey that is unpredictable and, at times, dark and mysterious. Two people undertaking such a trip together need to establish and maintain clear limits and boundaries to prevent themselves from getting derailed. This forms the topic of the next chapter.

2. Boundaries

I never, or almost never, occupy the middle of my cage;
my whole being surges towards the bars

André Paul Guillaume Gide (1869-1951)

As human enterprises, dynamic psychotherapy and psychoanalysis are intensely paradoxical at their base. On the one
hand, they are grounded in theoretical formulations regarding development, mental functioning, psychopathology and technique.
On the other hand, they involve a deep and sustained emotional
relationship between two individuals. It is this central paradox that
dictates that, in the conduct of these treatments, deliberateness and
spontaneity, knowledge and surprise, and discipline and freedom
co-exist in a gestalt of harmony. (For more on this matter, see Par-
sons, 2001.) Clearly, such a complex 'game' cannot be played without an agreed-upon guidelines and framework. The concept of
'boundaries' enters the discourse at this point.

In this chapter I will elucidate this concept in some detail. I will
categorize the plethora of notions that pervade this realm into
boundaries of three types: intrapersonal (intrapsychic), personal,
and interpersonal. This centripetal movement of discourse will
bring up the concept of 'optimal distance' (Bouvet, 1955; Balint,
1959; Mahler et al., 1975; Akhtar, 1992b), its potential overlap with
'interpersonal boundaries', and the cultural variations and psychopathology of boundaries and distance. Following this, I will address the various types of boundary violations and also note ways

41

to prevent such mishaps and to deal with their socio-clinical after-math.[9] My discussion of technical matters, however, will not be re-stricted to this aspect of boundaries. I will also describe the mea-sures needed to set up a clear and firm therapeutic frame from the outset and to safeguard it from major encroachments by transfer-ence and countertransference distortions.

INTRAPSYCHIC, PERSONAL AND INTERPERSONAL BOUNDARIES

The term 'boundaries' is used in psychoanalytic literature in three different ways: (i) intrapsychic boundaries, (ii) personal bound-aries, and (iii) interpersonal boundaries. Each of these categories has its developmental origins, phenomenological subtleties, cultur-al and pathological variants, and implications for technique. How-ever, these concepts overlap each other and the following elucida-tion of them in separate sections is a transparent artifice in the ser-vice of didactic clarity.

Intrapsychic Boundaries

Although Freud's (1900) early topographic model (dividing the mind into conscious, preconscious and unconscious systems) and later structural model (with entities like id, ego and superego) both implied separation barriers within the mind itself, the term 'boundaries' was not used by him. It appeared, with a prefix, as 'ego boundaries' for the first time in a paper by Tausk (1918). Later it was popularized by Federn (1952) who described 'inner ego boundaries 'as barriers that separate the ego from other mental structures. Klein's (1935, 1940) and Fairbairn's (1952) models of en-dopsychic structure also contained splits, schisms, and sequestered schemas within the mind.

   With Hartmann's (1950) differentiation between 'ego' and 'self' and Jacobson's (1964) refinement of 'self' as 'self-representation', the concept of boundaries came to be understood somewhat differ-ently. Jacobson (1964) proposed that the initial intrapsychic struc-ture is a fused self-object representation that evolves through pri-mary libidinal identifications with the mother. Gradually, differen-tiation between self- and object-representations begins. The propensity for their defensive re-fusion exists and is intensified by the presence of too much aggression within a psychic economy: this can lay the foundation of a psychotic core. Under loving circumstances, the self- and object-representation differentiation continues and is followed by the synthesis of 'good' and 'bad' self-representations into a composite self-representation and of 'good' and 'bad' object-representations into a composite internal object representation. These intrapsychic clusters are the metapsychological counterparts of identity formation (Kernberg, 1975, 1976). Here Erikson's (1950, 1956) work is pertinent. Besides emphasizing the synthesis of sequestered ego (self) fragments, Erikson underscored the importance of bringing together the past, present, and (wished-for) future views of the self; temporal continuity and continuity amidst change was seen by him as the hallmark of healthy identity.

Personal Boundaries

The boundaries of the self as a distinct organism have been described from various perspectives. Freud's (1895) *Reizchutz* or 'protective shield' is perhaps the earliest concept in this realm. Under this rubric, Freud proposed the existence of a threshold of a stimulation by the external environment, the exceeding of which becomes psychologically traumatic. Later authors (Mahler, 1958; Khan, 1963; Gediman, 1971; Esman, 1983) expanded Freud's views to include the regulation of internal stimuli also among the functions of this structure; Rapaport's (1951) term 'stimulus barrier' thus became synonymous with Freud's (1895) protective shield. The origins of such a barrier were traced to mother-infant interactions whereby the mother regulates the stimulation her infant has to face. This maternal function is gradually internalized by the child who then develops self-regulatory capacity with regards to the tolerable amounts of excitement, activity, and stimulation.

Tausk's (1918) 'ego boundaries' and Federn's (1952) 'external ego boundaries that separate ego from the external reality' are also important concepts in this regard. These authors, however, did not regard such boundaries as static and rigid. Their 'soft' notions were gradually replaced, as Gabbard and Lester (1995) note in their comprehensive review of the topic, by reified concepts. Reich's (1933) description of 'character armor', Bick's (1958) 'skin around the ego' and Anzieu's (1990) 'psychic envelopes' are among the most prominent illustrations of this tendency. The psychiatric 'necessity' of distinguishing between psychotic and non-psychotic conditions, both in the form of their flagrant 'state' and their subterranean 'trait' (Frosch, 1988a, 1988b) further consolidated the view that neat demarcations between self and non-self were possible and even desirable. Winnicott's (1953) delineation of the 'intermediate area of experience' and Searles' (1960) views about man's relationship with his non-human environment are prominent exceptions to this rigid me-not-me separation.

Interpersonal Boundaries

Psychoanalysts studying developmental processes (e.g. Mahler, 1958, 1971, 1972; Mahler et al., 1975; Winnicott, 1967, 1969, 1971; Tyson, 2005, 2006; Parens, 1979, 2006) invariably posit a view of boundaries as evolving from a 'dual unity' or 'symbiosis' or 'merger experiences' between two persons—i.e. mother and child.[10] Their models thus lay down the prototype for the interpersonal blurring of boundaries which, during adult life, can be accentuated by pathology or, in moderation, capitalized by the developmentally advanced capacities of mutuality (Bergman, 1980), collaborative work, love, sexual excitement (Kernberg, 1977, 1995) and friendship. Marital relationships especially test the resilience of the core self and flexibility of its outer boundaries.

This brings up the related issue of boundary-permeability, to which is relevant the work of Landis (1970) and Hartmann (1991), who described 'permeable' or 'impermeable' or 'thin' and 'thick' boundaries, respectively, as a broad way of organizing clusters of personality traits. Those with 'thin' boundaries displayed suggestibility, weakness of identity, and inconsistent defenses and behaviors. Those with 'thick' boundaries had stable identity and consistent behavior; they were also firm and assertive in interpersonal transactions. While constitutional factors did play a role here, the 'thickness' of boundaries showed a correlation with strong identification with the same-sex parent. It was also noted that if boundaries become 'too thick', rigidity and smugness results and if they become 'too thin' intense vulnerability to narcissistic injury and shame follows.

In sum, the term 'boundaries' seems to have intrapsychic referents (keeping mental contents or structures apart), personal referents (differentiating self from non-self), and interpersonal referents (regulating the impact of interacting with others). This last-mentioned emphasis upon the concept of boundaries is especially evi-

amazon.com

Billing Address
BArbara G Deutsch, MD
83 Fernwood Lane
Roslyn, New York 11576
United States

Shipping Address
BArbara G Deutsch, MD
83 Fernwood Lane
Roslyn, New York 11576
United States

SDthVgkRgR

Returns Are Easy!

Visit http://www.amazon.com/returns to return any item - including gifts - in unopened or original condition within 30 days for a full refund (other restrictions apply). Please have your order ID ready.

Your order of January 15, 2010 (Order ID 002-2015262-6852259)

Qty.	Item	Item Price	Total
1	Game Change: Obama and the Clintons, McCain and Palin, and the Race of a Lifetime Heilemann, John --- Hardcover (** P-1-P57D19 **) 0061733636	$15.39	$15.39
1	Turning Points in Dynamic Psychotherapy: Initial Assessment, Boundaries, Money, Disruptions and Suicidal Crises Akhtar, Salman --- Paperback (** P-4-B168D32 **) 185575811	$24.28	$24.28

Subtotal	$39.67
Tax	$3.42
Order Total	$43.09
Balance due	$0.00

A1

This shipment completes your order.

Have feedback on how we packaged your order? Tell us at www.amazon.com/packaging.

5/DthVgkRgR/-2 of 2-//PCP/second/5844781/0116-13:30/0115-19:07/sp117344482/1-1

dent in the psychoanalytically informed literature on marital and family therapy (Sholevar, 1985, 1995) and, in an even broader way, in the psychoanalytically informed writings on ethnic conflict resolution (Volkan, 1988, 1997). Finally, it should be noted that the psychotherapeutic (or psychoanalytic) situation—with its fixed length of sessions, predictable rhythm of appointments and payments, relative anonymity of the therapist, abstinence, and neutrality—is a highly special set-up of interpersonal boundaries. It is a context that requires firm limits on the one hand, and, on the other, being subject to intersubjective processes like empathy and projective identification allows subtle and transitory mergers of two minds. The work that goes on in this situation tests all boundaries regardless of their being intrapsychic, personal, or interpersonal.

THE RELATED CONCEPT OF OPTIMAL DISTANCE

The term 'optimal distance' was introduced into psychoanalytic literature by Bouvet (1958). In a paper titled 'Technical variation and the concept of distance', he defined 'distance' as 'the gap that separates the way in which a subject expresses his instinctual drives from how he would express them if the process of "handling" or "managing" these expressions did not intervene' (p. 211). Bouvet went on to explain that this 'managing' represents an aspect of the ego defense, and 'draws attention to the exterior aspect of the ego's activity, while "defense" characterizes more particularly its internal aspect' (p. 211).

A peculiar tension seems to exist in this definition. On the one hand, by regarding the gap between two manners of drive discharge as its cardinal characteristic, Bouvet posits an intrapsychic definition of the word 'distance'. On the other hand, by focusing on 'managing' or the 'exterior' aspect rather than on 'defense' or the 'internal' aspect of the ego's activity, Bouvet leans toward an interpersonal definition of distance. This stance is more apparent in the following passage from the same paper.

> The distance that a patient will take from his analyst varies constantly during the analysis, but in general it tends to diminish as the analysis progresses, until it disappears. It is this point which I call the *rapprocher*

(which signifies in French 'drawing close', but pro-
gressively). Once attained, this partial *rapprocher* can
be jeopardized by other conflicts, but appears to be
more easily reestablished, and to lead finally to a more
general *rapprocher*. (pp. 211-212)

The same intrapsychic-interpersonal tension in the definition of
'distance' is evident in the writings of Mahler (1971; Mahler et al.,
1975). She begins her view of 'distance' as being within the largely
interpersonal mother-child matrix but ends up with an internalized capacity for establishing optimal distance—in other words,
with an ego-attribute. 'Optimal distance' for her is 'a position between mother and child that best allows the infant to develop
those faculties which he needs in order to grow, that is, to individ-
uate' (Mahler et al., 1975, p. 291). This distance varies from one
phase of development to the other. In the symbiotic phase, the optimal distance is pretty much zero. In differentiation phase, it reaches its zenith. In the rapprochement sub-phase (from eighteen to
twenty-four months) no distance appears satisfactory as there is intense conflict between progressive drives for self-expression and
separation on the one hand, and regressive wishes for closeness
and merger on the other. Only after this phase is traversed with the
help of a tolerant and loving mother does the capacity for self and
object constancy appear. The ability to maintain optimal distance
from love-objects now develops. This definition is an obviously interpersonal one.

In other writings, however, Mahler takes a more intrapsychic
perspective referring to the distance 'between the self and the object world' (1975, p. 193). That she means internalized objects here
is confirmed by the very next sentence, which refers to the

oscillation between longing to merge with the good
object representation, with the erstwhile (in one's fantasy at least) blissful union with the symbiotic mother
and the defense against re-engulfment by her (which
causes loss of autonomous self identity). (1975, p. 193)

The symbiotic and practicing phase described by Mahler (1965,
1971; Mahler et al., 1975) have a close correspondence with Balint's

(1959) 'ocnophilia' and 'philobatism', respectively. The ocnophilic world consists of objects separated by horrid spaces and the philobatic world of friendly expanses dotted with unpredictable objects. The ocnophil lives from object to object, cutting short his travels through empty spaces. The philobat lives in cordial spaces, avoiding contact with dangerous objects. The ocnophil is a homebody, the philobat an eternal vagabond. Balint traced the ocnophilic tendency to the early tactile contact with mother and the philobatic bent to the latter separation-tolerant, visual contact with the mother. His acknowledgment that the two tendencies always co-exist parallels Mahler's (1972) recognition of 'man's eternal struggle against both fusion and isolation' (p. 130).

One thing is clear. All three authors dealing with distance (Bouvet, Mahler and Balint) imply that it is a Janus-faced concept with both intrapsychic and interpersonal referents. One way out of this paradox is to use the concept only in one particular context at a time. Thus in describing an individual's character, 'optimal distance' is best used in its intrapsychic sense i.e. as an ego-capacity. And, in describing the individual's relationships, therapeutic or otherwise, the term is best used in its interpersonal sense. However, this does not seem entirely satisfactory since both intrapsychic and interpersonal dimensions are active in all circumstances at the same time. This is most clear in the course of development when the intrapersonal is on the way to becoming intrapsychic and that, in turn, is tried out in the interpersonal realm. The best way out of this conundrum is, I believe, to accept the paradox and to regard the dialectical tension between the two perspectives (intrapsychic and interpersonal) as being inherent to the concept. Finally, it should be added that the vicissitudes of the Oedipus complex also contribute to the capacity to maintain optimal distance. Exclusion from parental sexuality and acceptance of generational boundaries are cardinal achievements of this phase (Freud, 1924). However, this does not imply complete sensual and aggressive disjunction between generations.

Putting everything together, it appears that at the preoedipal level, optimal distance refers to a psychic position that permits intimacy with others without loss of autonomy and separateness without painful aloneness. At the oedipal level, optimal distance can be viewed as the capacity to renounce primary oedipal objects in a way that (on the aggressive side) permits individual autonomy without sacrifice of traditional continuity and (on the libidinal side) establishment of the incest barrier without total obliteration of aim-inhibited, cross-generational eroticism.

This makes it abundantly clear that the 'interpersonal boundaries' and 'optimal distance' are, in some ways, conceptual twins. Both refer to the ego's modulation of relationship between self and others. Both are developmentally derived, though might also have some constitutional substrate. Both are, to a greater or lesser extent, products of modal child-rearing, hence culture-bound.

CULTURAL VARIATIONS

The clarity, firmness, and permeability of boundaries are governed not only by constitutional and psychological factors, but by the culture-at-large as well. While it is easy to see how child-rearing patterns in one or the other society might uphold this or that degree of psychic separateness and autonomy as being desirable, the fact that psychically extraneous variables (e.g. density of population, means of communication and travel) and one's large group's history, literature, and mythology can also affect personal and interpersonal boundaries often comes as a surprise to mental health practitioners. Take, for instance, intrapsychic boundaries, especially those keeping the conscious secondary process mental contents separate from the primary process material of the unconscious. Comparing a group of poets and artists with a group of bankers and surgeons on this parameter alone would readily reveal that the optimal conscious-unconscious separation differs greatly between them. The former have much greater access to their unconscious goings-on and are more comfortable with the seemingly inexplicable messages from the vaults of their psyche. Modal prototypes of intrapsychic boundaries clearly differ in these groups.

A psychically autonomous and separate self is also not universal. Such a structure is the end-product, or at least the desired end-product, of the childhood separation-individuation process (Mahler et al., 1975) and its re-working during adolescence (Blos, 1967) in the Western Anglo-Saxon culture. To regard this developmental trajectory as ubiquitous to human experience betrays psychoanalytic colonialism. Careful observation of mother-child interactions in India and Japan, experience of treatment of children and adolescents from those cultures, and reconstructions in the analyses of adults living there (Carstairs, 1957; Roland, 1998; Kakar, 1985; Freeman, 1998; Bonovitz, 1998) have revealed that the clearly demarcated 'psychoanalytic self' is not the modal psychic structure. Instead of an individualized self, the prevalent psychic organization is one of 'familial self' (Roland, 1988). Such a self is characterized by intense emotional connectedness and reciprocity with others and draws its narcissistic sustenance from 'strong identification with the reputation and honor of the family and other groups' (p. 8). Its modes of cognition and relating are highly context-bound and differ from the individualistic and autonomous self typically seen in the West, especially North America.

The degree to which an individual's self remains permeable to influence from others, especially one's elders, also varies from culture to culture. Writing of Indian patients, for instance, Kakar (1985) states that

> the relational orientation is still the 'natural' way of viewing the self and the world. Thus it is not uncommon for family members, who often (and significantly!) accompany the patient for the first interview, to complain about the patient's autonomy as one of the symptoms of his disorder. (p. 446)

The emphasis in such cultures is upon inter-dependence and not upon autonomy. Friendships are deep. People take all sorts of relatives into account while making important life decisions. 'Infantile objects are relinquished very gradually and this process does not take place to the degree necessary in cultures where the child is being prepared to live an adult life that is independent of the extended family' (Bonovitz, 1998, p. 182). Not surprisingly, the view of what is 'optimal distance' between two individuals (and their psyches) also varies in these cultures. This effects what is felt to be the normal frequency of contact between relatives and friends, the extent of intimacy in relationships, and even the amount of physical contact between people.

All four variables mentioned above (i.e. the porous versus closed nature of intrapsychic boundaries, individual versus famil-

ial self, relational versus autonomous orientation and average-ex-
pectable optimal distance) impact upon the conduct of cross-cultural psychotherapy and psychoanalysis. Overlooking this can lead
to assumptions and interventions that result in hurting the patient
and/or creating falsehood in the therapeutic alliance.

PSYCHOPATHOLOGY

Psychopathology often involves disturbances of boundaries. In
fact, the more severe the psychopathology, the greater is the disturbance of boundaries. This applies to all three realms (i.e., intrapsychic, personal, and interpersonal) of boundaries. A few examples
should suffice to illustrate this proposition.

   Intrapsychic boundaries between various psychic structures
(e.g., between id and ego, between ego and superego, and between
ego and ego-ideal) are affected in a number of ways by psychopathology. Schizophrenic psychoses, for instance, involve a diminished demarcation between id and ego. The primary process
begins to alter thinking; wishes and dreads of the inner world
come to dominate the ego's perception of external reality. Another
situation where collapse of intrapsychic boundaries is evident is
narcissistic and hypomanic character pathology. The usual gap between ego and ego-ideal closes in these conditions resulting in confusion between real and wishful self-perceptions; boastfulness,
cockiness, and irreverence are the behavioral counterparts of this.
Yet another situation is the fusion between a harsh superego and
the ego, leading to the syndrome of 'messianic sadism' (Akhtar,
2007) where malignant prejudice and cruelty towards others becomes morally sanctified.

   In contrast to such intrapsychic boundary dissolutions are
states characterized by the cropping up of abnormal barriers between clusters of mental content. The syndrome of identity diffusion (Kernberg, 1975, 1984; Akhtar, 1984) that underlies severe personality disorders and the defensive separation of self-representations in 'dissociative character' (Brenner, 1994, 2001) are prime examples of this type of intrapsychic boundary proliferation. Contradictory self-states, including those representing different eras of
life, exist in sequestered form without being synthesized into a
composite whole.

On the outer rind of personality, the boundaries that separate self from non-self also show alterations in states of psychopathology. In psychoses and 'psychotic characters' (Frosch 1988a, 1988b; Volkan & Akhtar, 1997; Akhtar, 1997), blurring of such demarcations is a central feature. In the 'as-if' personality (Deutsch, 1942), the permeability of personal boundaries is greatly increased resulting in rapid identifications with others which are 'lost' with a comparable ease. The exact opposite is true of bull-headed narcissistic and paranoid characters who refuse to be influenced by anyone, or of those with Asperger syndrome (Wing, 1981) who remain peculiarly disconnected and cold in their interactions.

This brings up the psychopathology of 'optimal distance'. While agoraphobia, claustrophobia, and difficulties in adjusting to a marital relationship are often the result of conflicts over optimal distance, it is in the setting of severe personality disorders that distance related problems become most evident. For individuals with these conditions, involvement with others stirs up a characteristic 'need-fear dilemma' (Burnham et al., 1969): to be intimate is to risk engulfment and to be apart is to court aloneness. This can lead to various compromise solutions. The borderline continues to go back and forth (Akhtar, 1990; Gunderson, 1985; Melges & Swartz, 1989). The narcissist can sustain allegiances longer and shows such oscillations in 'slow motion' (Adler, 1981; Kernberg, 1970). The paranoid bristles at any change in distance initiated by others, preferring the 'reliability' of his fear of being betrayed (Blum, 1981). The schizoid opts for withdrawal on the surface while maintaining an intense imaginative tie to his objects (Akhtar, 1987; Fairbairn, 1952; Guntrip, 1969). The anti-social and the hypomanic, though internally uncommitted, develop swift intimacy with others. In essence, all severe personality disorders show impairment of the capacity to maintain optimal distance. Their problems are gross, however. More subtle anxieties in this realm, accompanied by fantasies of 'tethers, orbits, and invisible fences' (Akhtar, 1992b) surrounding one, can exist in less disturbed individuals. These are often discernible only during the work of in-depth psychotherapy or psychoanalysis.

B̲OUNDARY V̲IOLATIONS

Though transgressions of the therapeutic frame occurred from the earliest days of psychoanalysis and psychodynamic therapy[11], the term 'boundary violations' itself gained popularity only after the seminal book by Gabbard and Lester (1995). According to them, 'boundary violations' refer to egregious enactments on the therapist's part that are harmful to the patient. While such acts can emanate from predatory and psychopathic tendencies on the therapist's part, most times their occurrence is a matter of psychodynamic 'co-creation' by the patient and the therapist.[12] In other words, it is the unchecked interplay of transference and countertransference that leads to boundary violations.

Gabbard and Lester (1995) emphasize that behaviors constituting 'boundary violations' differ from those subsumed under the term 'boundary crossings'. There are four distinctions between them:

- 'Boundary crossings' involve a transient blurring of the selves of patient and therapist and the resulting proneness to enactment is caught 'mid-way' by the therapist. He then reflects upon what was about to happen and uses that knowledge for the advancement of therapy. In contrast, 'boundary violations' are characterized by a loss of self-reflection on the therapist's part. Consequently, such behaviors destroy the viability of treatment.

- 'Boundary crossings' are enactments that are discussed by both therapist and patient whereas 'boundary violations' are typically placed outside of the context of therapy. It is as if those behaviors (e.g. hand-holding, kissing) had nothing to do with the treatment that is being carried on.

- 'Boundary crossings' are generally responded to by the therapist and patient by reflection and attempts to understand what just took place. 'Boundary violations', in contrast, are unresponsive to the therapist's own efforts to understand and control them. There is also an aura of secrecy about such acts.

- 'Boundary violations', in contrast to 'boundary crossings', are exploitative of the patient and are harmful to the treatment process. There is a profound neglect of the patient's interests on the therapist's part. At times, there might even be a deliberate attempt to manipulate and hurt the patient.

Subtle overlaps between the two concepts notwithstanding, this view of 'boundary violation' prepares one to observe, record, and reflect upon their occurrence in a variety of realms as the treatment process unfolds.

Sexual Boundary Violations

In the course of intensive psychotherapy, one frequently encounters 'erotic' (Freud, 1915) and 'erotized' (Blum, 1973; Akhtar, 1994, 1996) transferences. The former emanates from unresolved oedipal longings and is generally subtle in expression. The latter arises from oral hunger, carries more explicit sexual demands, and has a coercive nature. The therapist dealing with the former begins to feel enthusiasm towards the patient. The therapist dealing with the latter feels burdened and manipulated. Paradoxically, then, the patient who is less stridently demanding of sexual involvement with the therapist gives rise to a more 'real' erotic counter-resonance in the therapist. The risk of the therapist developing a 'love-sickness' (Twemlow & Gabbard, 1989; Gabbard & Lester, 1995) is great under such circumstances.

A number of other variables contribute to the therapist finding himself on the 'slippery slope' of countertransference acting out. The most common scenarios causing this are the following:

- The therapist of an abused female patient might be under the sway of 'disidentification with the aggressor' (Gabbard, 1997) whereby he might disavow any (transference) connection with the patient's abusers and try to be at the utmost kind and indulgent towards her. Consequently he might make heroic efforts to 'help' the patient and, in the process, transgress boundaries (e.g. by hugging and kissing the patient).

- The therapist and patient might act out their repressed oedipal fantasies. 'The female patient may have harbored a childhood fantasy that she was somehow taking care of her depressed father in despair over an empty marriage. The analyst, on the other hand, may be unconsciously rescuing his depressed mother to heal the patient. Female patients who have childhood suffered trauma may be particularly appealing to the love-sick analyst who is intent upon rescue' (Gabbard, 2006, p. 42).

- A male therapist might mistake his female patient's desire for maternal tenderness and nurturance for sexual advance and, in a state of personal vulnerability, succumb to the temptations this causes in him.

Sexual boundary violations are more likely to occur if the patient has been sexually abused as a child and is re-creating a similar situation though, of course, with the hope that a repetition of early trauma will not occur this time. The likelihood of violations markedly increases if the therapist is characterologically unable to handle erotic countertransference or has become so due to romantic and sexual deprivation in his current life (Gabbard & Lester, 1995; Celenza, 2007).

Narcissistic Boundary Violations

Though the therapist's misuse of the power difference in the dyad does contribute to sexual boundary violations, there are egregious behaviors where themes of domination, subjugation and control occupy the center stage. Naming them 'narcissistic boundary violations', Levine (2005) underscores the role of self-aggrandizement in them. Haughty disregard of the patient's autonomy, taking over the daily conduct of his life, advising him to marry this or divorce that person are all manifestations of such violations. This may result from the therapist acting out a particular countertransference stimulated by the patient. More often, it emanates from the therapist's narcissistic character pathology even if that is brought into play, at a given time, by a patient's 'seductions'.

CLINICAL VIGNETTE 6

Bill Silverberg had been in intensive treatment with a highly charismatic therapist known for his stylish clothes and expensive cars. The therapy floundered.

Bill dropped out and, a few years later, his therapist passed away. Six months later, Bill entered into treatment with me.

A highly masochistic man with a tall and lanky frame, Bill had a 'father problem'. On the one hand, he despised his father for constantly ridiculing him during his childhood. On the other hand, he was dependent upon the old man's financial largesse. Unable to make ends meet on his own, Bill received a monthly stipend from his wealthy father. His treatment with me was characterized by a powerful father transference in which he attempted to both flatter and devalue me. Praising me to great extent, he would defeat all interpretations by turning them into trite witticisms. Gradually, however, I learned that this sadomasochistic game was actually an advance over his original tendency to be utterly subservient to authority figures.

Now a memory from his previous treatment emerged. Bill told me that once he was going to Napa Valley, California, and mentioned it to his therapist. The latter responded by not only giving him tips about the wineries to visit but by talking about his own extensive (and expensive!) wine collection. Bill brought back a bottle of wine to his therapist as a gift. It was accepted without question. This soon became a pattern. Bill would bring wine for his therapist who would take it without any question or discussion. Then one day, Bill brought a case of wine bottles for his therapist who gave him his car keys and asked Bill to put it in the trunk of his car before starting the session!

The enactment of narcissistic-masochistic (and homosexual) transference-countertransference fantasies is clearly evident here. What is disturbing though is not the patient's 'seductions' and submission but the therapist's nonchalance and smug exploitation of his patient.

Cultural Boundary Violations

With the changing demography of patients and therapists nation-wide, the likelihood of the two partners in the clinical dyad belonging to different ethnic, racial, religious, and linguistic backgrounds has increased. With this, the potential of 'cultural boundary violations' (Akhtar, 2007b) has grown by leaps and bounds. These involve situations where the therapist imposes his or her values regarding a wide range of sociocultural matters upon the patient, causing the latter to suffer unnecessary confusion and iatrogenic conflict. For example: How often should an adult offspring call his out-of-town mother on the phone? Should premarital sex be a necessary step before the decision to get engaged and married?

'Cultural boundary violations' are also caused by the therapist ignoring that such boundaries even exist. Treating immigrant and racially different patients with no attention at all to their cultural backgrounds constitutes a situation of this sort.[13] Pronouncing the name of an immigrant patient or of his hometown in one's own way without asking the patient's guidance about the correct way of saying them is a more subtle form of 'cultural boundary violations' based upon a colonial mentality. Insistence upon an illusory cultural oneness is, in the end, more harmful than reassuring to the patient.

Miscellaneous Boundary Violations

There are other transgressions, besides those mentioned above, which can harm the patient. Prominent among such boundary violations are the following: (i) asking the patient to donate money for causes of interest to the therapist[14] or seeking the patient's help in a financial venture, (ii) seeing more than one family member in intensive psychotherapy or psychoanalysis simultaneously, (iii) disregarding the patient's realities (e.g. lack of money, too much distance from the therapist's office) and making the patient feel guilty for being unable to comply with the therapist's 'recommendation' for money and frequency of visits, and (iv) revealing stimulating information about one's self (e.g. one's childhood trauma, details of one's romantic life) to the patient; this almost invariably burdens and traumatizes the patient. The common elements in these acts are the therapist's thoughtlessness, selfishness, and exploitation of the patient.

TECHNICAL IMPLICATIONS

Having covered the concept of boundaries and optimal distance, their cultural and psychopathological variations, and the different types of boundary violations that can occur in the course of treatment, we can now turn our attention to the technical implications of these observations. As we do so, we become ever more aware of how important the 'trio of guideposts' (Pine, 1997, p. 13) of anonymity, neutrality, and abstinence is for the conduct of dynamic psychotherapy and psychoanalysis. Furthermore, we discern six areas of technical concern in the realm of boundaries and distance. These include: (i) beginning treatment with a well-established framework, (ii) recognizing risk factors for future boundary violations, (iii) maintaining and safeguarding boundaries during treatment, (iv) monitoring one's countertransference, (v) seeking supervisory and collegial input, and (vi) dealing with the aftermath of boundary violations.

Beginning Treatment With A Well-Defined Framework

It is important to set a clear, firm and well-defined therapeutic framework from the very outset. While no actual data is available, it is my impression that psychotherapists in training are often not taught the importance of this matter. Consequently they go into the world of clinical practice and take on patients in psychotherapy without setting up explicit guidelines and boundaries of the treatment; many subsequent stalemates are the result of this initial omission.

I, for one (and I am sure there are many others like me in this regard), try to set aside one session *after* the initial assessment is over and the patient and I have decided to work together and *before* the psychotherapy or psychoanalysis proper has begun (though, of course, I am aware of the potential dynamic reverberations of this session as well), for going over the various rules, guidelines, and expectations for our work together. This prevents later misunderstandings and sets the ground for seeing departures from it as resistance and acting out. I have found it useful to go over the following points in this 'frame-setting' session.

- Telling the patient the desired frequency of sessions and working out an agreement concerning it.

- Letting the patient know the exact duration of each session, adding that if I were late by 1-2 minutes I would acknowledge it, and offer to see the patient for the full time provided he or she could stay longer.

- Going over the fee and the method of billing and collection in a clear manner one more time.

- Making one's policy for payments for missed sessions clear to the patient. (See Chapter Three for details.)

- Informing the patient of the location of restrooms, water fountains and public telephones in the building. Also, pointing out the ever-present box of tissues so that if the patient ever needs it, he does not have to ask or search for it.

- Establishing a method of emergency communication so that should either party urgently need to leave a message for the other, it would be possible to do so.

- Explaining the need of regularity and continuity of sessions adding that both parties should strive to assure the least amount of time is missed from their work. However, the therapist should let the patient know that he is aware that, at times, the patient's vacations might not correspond with his and this is certainly acceptable.

- Laying out clearly the work expected from the patient during the hour. For dynamic psychotherapy this might consist of saying the following: 'What I expect you to do is to talk as freely as you can about the problems and difficulties that are affecting you at the time of our session; or, if there are no particular problems or difficulties affecting you at the time, to talk as freely as you can about everything that is on your mind. That may include thoughts and memories and perceptions, dreams and feelings, and questions. The more openly and freely you talk about yourself, the more you try to communicate fully what is on your mind to the limits of your own awareness, the better. When one talks freely about what come to mind, important issues tend to emerge naturally. Thus, regardless of whether what comes to mind seems important or trivial, it will help in the long run if you go ahead and talk about it' (Kernberg et al., 1990, p. 27). One might also add a comment about the expected development of transference and the need to discuss it openly. This might serve as an orienting device and a gentle push towards candor, especially for patients with less than optimal psychological mindedness. This comment might go like this: 'As our work proceeds, you might begin to develop some feelings, curiosities, and fantasies about me. This is natural and expected in any sustained dialogue between two people. What is different here is that you are expected to talk about all such feelings and fantasies, since these too might give us clues to the nature of the difficulties that have brought you here. Talking about them, therefore, will also be a facet of your treatment.'[15]

- Clarifying one's own role to the patient by saying that the therapist's task will be to help the patient gain understanding of himself, that the therapist will be listening to what the patient is saying, and that he will make comments when he has something significant to contribute. The therapist should also tell the patient that he will treat the latter's questions like any other of his thoughts. Consequently, he may not answer them factually; his silence in this regard would be an invitation to the patient to explore what in his mind gave rise to the question in the first place.

- Answering the patient's questions regarding the above-mentioned points in a straightforward and factual manner without mystifying the patient by interpreting the reasons behind such questions.

These guidelines orient the patient and therapist to the reality framework of therapy within which the unfolding of transference, countertransference and reminiscence-based emotions in general takes place. At the same time such orientation is not once and for all; the risk of violating boundaries and collapsing optimal distance is ever present in treatment and this necessitates constant attention to such matters.

Recognizing Risk Factors For Future Boundary Violations

In a book dealing comprehensively with sexual boundary violations, Celenza (2007) has identified eight features of the therapist's personality that may make it difficult for him to maintain proper boundaries during the treatment. These include: (i) chronic narcissistic neediness, (ii) covert grandiosity and the tendency to regard oneself as an 'exception' (Freud, 1916), (iii) intolerance of negative transference, (iv) childhood background of emotional neglect on the one hand and of a highly sexualized relationship with the primary caregiver on the other, (v) history of moral transgressions (e.g., incest, infidelity) by parents which create 'superego lacunae' (Johnson & Szurek, 1952) in the offspring, (vi) anger towards authority figures, (vii) restricted fantasy life, and (viii) tendency to circumvent unconscious countertransference through the misuse of conscious countertransference 'love'.

This list is especially impressive since it links characterological factors in the therapist with the developments in the treatment and is based upon data derived from interviews as well psychological testing of transgressive therapists. Keeping these factors in mind while selecting candidates for training and while supervising those who have already become therapists can help detect difficulty in boundary maintenance in its nascent stages. Therapists themselves might benefit by looking over this list and in a move of truthfulness and genuine soul-searching see if aspects of this profile fit them and, if so, seek (further) personal treatment and develop extra vigilance towards the potential impact of their vulnerabilities upon their work.

Besides the variables related to the therapist, certain features in the patient's psychopathology also increase the risk of boundary violations. This happens when a patient has an intense craving for oneness with the Other (Kogan, 2006). It also happens if the patient has been sexually abused as a child. Hoping to overcome the effects of such trauma, these patients tend to create situations which can get out of hand and end up re-traumatizing them. The earliest hints of this tendency are often discernible during the initial assessment of the patient.

CLINICAL VIGNETTE 7

Layla Aafandi, a thirty year-old pharmacist of Iranian origin, came to her first interview in a revealing dress. The neckline of her blouse swooped down to reveal a major portion of her breasts and her skirt was up to her mid-thigh region. Even more strikingly, she 'sat' on the chair in a nearly lying down posture. Her legs were extended and one of her feet came very close to mine. I was made uncomfortable by this and immediately suspected that she had been sexually abused as a child. However, I did not pull my foot back quickly. I waited, and went on to hear her story and collect pertinent information. Soon the history of childhood sexual abuse (by her father) came out. At this point, I gently withdrew my foot and pointed out that her manner of sitting, which created the possibility of physical contact between us, was related to what had happened in her past. I added that she was unconsciously inducing the discomfort of unwelcome proximity in me so that I could emotionally know what she had felt as a child. Besides, it seemed that she was also testing the safety of being with me. These remarks led to her sitting up, crying, and gradually revealing a long history of sexual exploitation, including two rapes, during adult life.

This account of risk factors emanating from therapist and patient addresses the possibility of sexual boundary violations. It does not address the issue of 'cultural boundary violations'. Here the guidelines I earlier evolved for therapists to achieve and sustain 'cultural neutrality' (Akhtar, 1999, pp.113-116) become pertinent. Essentially, these consist of the therapist's: (i) personal treatment to mitigate paranoid defenses, (ii) study of the interface of social anthropology with clinical work, (iii) treating patients of many cultures, (iv) protecting his work ego from becoming narrowly provincial or excessively 'culturalized', and (v) leading an open and cosmopolitan life.

Maintaining and Safeguarding Boundaries During Treatment

As the treatment progresses, the therapist must keep an eye on how the various aspects of the agreed upon framework are being impacted upon by the patients evolving transferences and the regressions consequent upon them. Thus marked lateness for appointments, delay of payments, prolonged silences, and missed sessions etc., become legitimate topics for their investigation. Requests or demands for hand-holding, hugs, and other forms of physical contact[16] as well as the wish for interaction outside the treatment hours have to be similarly dealt with by firm containment and encouragement to explore what underlies them rather than gratification and alteration of the therapeutic limits and boundaries. In effect, the therapist cleans up the seepage of the patient's psychopathology onto the treatment frame by turning it into a topic for his curiosity and understanding.

Under fortunate circumstances, this clarifying and interpretive approach works. It reduces the pressure towards enactment and brings forth fresh material for consideration by both the patient and therapist (Casement, 1982). At other times, this does not seem to be enough and the therapist has to resort to firm limit-setting.

CLINICAL VIGNETTE 8

Tania Ruggeiro, a twenty-eight year-old doctoral candidate in psychology was in treatment with me. Having been abruptly abandoned by her father at age six and later sexually abused by her stepfather, she had grown to mistrust men and was deeply conflicted about her femininity. All this began to change as our work progressed.

Then, one day, she announced that she was applying for a job in the department where I worked, a job that would result in her having an office one or two rooms down the hallway from me. Exploration of the potential meanings of this desire led to its links with the 'shocks' she had received from both her real father and her stepfather. The element of projective identification whereby her experience of being a neglected and yet painfully over-stimulated child was being induced into me was obvious. Interpretations along this line were met by agreement but the resulting insight was soon submerged under the rationalization of finding such a good job. Pointing out the reality that such daily proximity might 'contaminate' our work was responded to by earnest promises to keep away from me. Failing all else and finding her intent upon taking this position, I had to tell her that she had a choice to make: either take the job or continue treatment with me. It was only then that she realized how serious the situation was and with sadness and some anger withdrew her application. More material began to emerge about her childhood trauma. including memories and affects that had hitherto remained unconscious.

Besides managing such gross encroachments upon personal and interpersonal boundaries, the therapist has to be mindful of not disturbing the patient's intrapsychic boundaries too much. Speaking while the patient is in a contemplative pause and making ill-timed, deep interpretations (regardless of their 'correctness') disregards the patient's need to be quiet or keep some things still unconscious, respectively. This sort of 'invisible boundary violation' (see Clinical Vignette 17) can traumatize the patient and should be avoided.

Monitoring One's Countertransference

The therapist must apply the principle of vigilance regarding boundaries and optimal distance to himself as well. Working intensively with patients mobilizes strong feelings and the therapist must allow himself to feel them and learn from them (Coen, 2002). The more he is able to do so, the less likely he would be to act them out. The novice often needs a senior practitioner's 'permission' to experience the wide range of affects, fantasies and impulses that arise during the clinical hour.[17]

The best recourse when countertransference pressure to act out is great is careful self-scrutiny, self-analysis, reading about the particular dynamic issue involved, and seeking therapeutic or supervisory consultation (see below). In addition, such impulses might also have to be dealt with by the old-fashioned methods of self-control, suppression (see Werman, 1983, for the ego-defensive functions of suppression), and mourning. This is, in part, the essence of the principle of 'abstinence', central to working deeply with patients.

CLINICAL VIGNETTE 9

As Rebecca Sherman began to 'heal' her intrapsychic split of being a horrible person and a truly noble soul, a passionate interest in zebras developed in her. Having come across a papier-mâché replica of the animal in a curiosity shop, she found herself magically captured by its predominant feature: the coexistence of black and white lines. She felt this represented her more integrated state and soon embarked on a collection of zebra replicas of all sorts.

Around this time, one day I was in a shop where I saw a beautiful little zebra and felt a strong urge to buy it for Rebecca. I wanted to give it to her during our next session. 'This will make her so happy,' I thought with pleasure. It would show her how attuned I was to her and this, in turn, would further her healing, I argued internally. But I tolerated not acting on my impulse (with some difficulty) and as the strong emotion passed, began to see how what Gabbard (1997) has called 'disidentification with the aggressor' (i.e. with the patient's bad internal objects) was at work here and I was about to take my first step on what frequently turns out to be a slippery slope. Further reflection revealed more dynamic issues within myself, some countertransference-related and others independently personal in nature.

Seeking Supervisory and Collegial Input

While psychotherapy relies upon confidentiality, the development of 'hyper-confidentiality' (Celenza, 2007) is undesirable. The latter involves the construction of a thick insulation around the treatment bubble which promotes secrecy and is impermeable to supervisory or collegial input. This is conducive to the occurrence of boundary violations in the treatment.

In a wise elucidation of this matter, Celenza (2007) emphasizes that it is inappropriate to conduct treatment without explicit reference to the fact that the process will be subject to periodic and anonymous review in supervision, case conferences, or peer groups. Not making this clear to the patient creates 'the illusion of an exclusive, closed system that is at best a fantasy and at worst a harmful reality' (p 188). Celenza takes the matter one step further by suggesting that

> in all therapies and analyses. We must make explicit the implicit spatial context at the beginning of the treatment and throughout—not just between therapist and patient but in real space, that is, in peer groups, consulting and/or supervisory contexts. When we begin a treatment, I suggest that we state explicitly to the patient that the process will be periodically discussed (confidentially and anonymously) with a consultant, peer group, and/or supervisor. What I suggest here is to make explicit that the therapeutic couple exists within a larger context and that this context will not be forgotten and that these ties and boundaries will not be severed. (p 188)

If the patient insists that the therapist must not consult with anyone about their work, the reasons underlying such a wish for secrecy (with all its attendant fantasies) should be actively explored. Clinical work must not be allowed to become a closed system and the prophylactic significance of supervision and peer group consultation must not be minimized.

Dealing With The Aftermath Of Boundary Violations

A boundary violation, especially one involving therapist-patient sexual intercourse, harms many people besides the two parties in the clinical dyad. Spouses are hurt, colleagues dismayed, and other patients of the therapist shocked (Ross, 1995). Ripples of mistrust and anger spread outwards, involving not only individuals but professional organizations and legal authorities. Keeping the broad reach of such fallout in mind necessitates that interventions be made at various levels and with various parties. Spouses and other 'unaffected' patients of the boundary-violating therapist might need serious clinical attention. The victim (patient) and the perpetrator (therapist) especially need help. Both might benefit from psychotherapeutic help that facilitates mourning and deepens the understanding of what happened and why. At times, a mediation process (Schoner et al., 1989) whereby a consultant, with expertise and knowledge about the emotional sequelae of sexual boundary violations, meets with the therapist and patient together. This might provide the opportunity for the perpetrator to overcome his denial and apologize to the victim. Individual interventions can follow this thawing encounter with reality.

The issues of subsequent therapy of the victim and the perpetrator are complex and beyond the scope of this chapter. These important matters, including the role of ethics committees, licensing boards, and legal system are discussed in meaningful detail by Gabbard and Lester (1995) and especially Celenza (2007) who focuses upon the rehabilitation of boundary violating therapists.

CONCLUDING REMARKS

In this chapter I have elucidated the concept of boundaries, noting their intrapsychic, personal, and interpersonal vicissitudes in some detail. I have also addressed the related concept of optimal distance. Highlighting the cultural variations of such psychic phenomena and the pathological configurations common in this realm has prepared the ground for my discussion of boundary violations. Adding to the sexual boundary violations already well discussed in the literature, I have described three other types of transgressions (narcissistic, cultural, and miscellaneous). In the technical section of the paper, I have outlined six important strategies, namely (i) recognizing risk factors, (ii) establishing clear boundaries from the start, (iii) maintaining and safeguarding the therapeutic framework, (iv) remaining vigilant towards countertransference developments, (v) keeping the therapeutic situation open to supervisory and collegial input, and (vi) dealing with the aftermath, in case a boundary violation does end up taking place. I have sought to anchor all this in theory though with little loss of attention to pragmatic issues.

One particular aspect of our clinical enterprise that I have only briefly touched upon here pertains to money. While personal boundaries do involve one's financial status and money-related dealings, and while boundary violations of the sort discussed in this chapter can involve money matters, the psychological significance of money far exceeds this narrow parameter of concern. Moreover, money is involved in the conduct of dynamic psychotherapy in more ways that one, as the following chapter demonstrates.

3. MONEY

Nearly a hundred years ago, Freud (1913) noted that most people approach matters of money with 'inconsistency, prudishness, and hypocrisy' (p. 131). Little has changed since then. It is still difficult for people to talk about their realities, fantasies, feelings, and aspirations involving money in a peaceful manner. This is not only because money is important in external reality but also because it has powerful meanings in the inner world of emotions. Not surprisingly, concerns about money readily become drawn into psychopathology and its treatment. The conceptual and technical knots in the encounter between money and psychotherapy have myriad forms indeed (Krueger, 1986a; Borneman, 1976; Rothstein, 1986).

In this chapter, I will attempt to shed light on these problems and their potential solutions. I will begin with a brief survey of literature on the symbolic significance of money and then delineate the psychopathological syndromes involving money.[18] My focus, however, will be upon how various aspects of our clinical work, including the therapeutic frame, transference, and countertransference are impacted upon by matters of money. Elucidation of these will lead me to explore the technical dilemmas rampant in this realm and suggest some ways of handling them.

69

PSYCHOLOGICAL SIGNIFICANCE OF MONEY

In a paper titled 'Character and Anal Erotism', Freud (1908) listed parsimony as a major trait of the obsessional personality. He traced the reluctance such individuals show in parting with money to the pleasure felt by the anal-phase child in retaining feces. Invoking illustrations from fairy tales, mythology, language, and dreams, Freud declared that money and feces were equated in the unconscious. He stated that two factors facilitate this equation. First, the striking contrast between a precious and a worthless substance makes the former a perfect disguise for the latter. Second,

> the original erotic interest in defecation is, as we know, destined to be extinguished in later years. In those years, the interest in money makes its appearance as new interest which has been absent in childhood. This makes it easier for the earlier impulsion, which is in the process of losing its aim, to be carried over to the newly emerging aim. (p. 175)

Freud's notions were phenomenologically embellished by his early pupils (Ferenczi, 1914; Jones, 1918; Fenichel, 1938, 1945) though with little addition to their theoretical basis. The feces-money equation thus became the established psychoanalytic dictum and miserliness was firmly ensconced as an anal trait.

However, as psychoanalytic motivational theory evolved from its instinctual foundations to include the ego, object-relational, and self-psychological perspectives, additional views regarding the emotional significance of money were voiced. Klein (1937) saw the origin of greed in the early oral phase and stated that its purpose was a hungry, destructive introjection of the frustrating breast. Money came to symbolize this elusive source of security later in life; children's fears of poverty betrayed the expectation of punishment over unmitigated hostile phantasies towards the mother. According to Klein, the adult depressive's dread of becoming destitute could be traced to this very dynamic of early childhood. Extension of her ideas was evident in Kernberg's (1975, 1976, 1984) descriptions of narcissistic personality that included the intense fervor with which some of these individuals pursue wealth. It was as if having money would provide assurance that one was not unloved and 'bad' (i.e. hostile). However, the goal of such contentment remains elusive and the narcissist keeps chasing it like a mirage.

The self-psychological perspective on money (Krueger, 1986b) emphasized the exhibitionistic aspect of wanting to be wealthy. Showing off one's financial success, with all its colorful accoutrements, provided a way to seek affirmation and applause from others. This helped maintain a positive self-image. It also provided a sense of vitality and coherence to an otherwise fragile self. Yet more psychological meanings of the interest in acquiring large sums of money were discerned over time (Blanton, 1976; Kaufman, 1976; Fuqua, 1986). These pertained to phallic competitiveness with one's rivals, sadistic wishes to triumph over one's 'enemies', and the 'some day...' (Akhtar, 1996) fantasy of leading an effortless and blissful existence by returning to the early infantile merger with mother. All in all, money seemed to acquire multiple symbolic functions and thus became vulnerable to being caught up in conflicts from diverse levels of development.

PSYCHOPATHOLOGICAL SYNDROMES INVOLVING MONEY

The flamboyant overspending of money in manic states and the delusional dread of poverty associated with profound depression (Slater & Roth, 1977; Wolpert, 1980; DSM-IV, 1990) are well-recognized monetary manifestations of psychopathology. Less known are the subtle ways in which psychological conflicts shape attitudes regarding money. The following six conditions stand out in this context.

Chronic Miserliness

That frequent topic of behind-the-back conversation, miserliness, is a Janus-faced problem with considerable intrapsychic and interpersonal ramifications. Before going into them, however, it should be emphasized that miserliness is unrelated to the actual financial state of the individual. Both the rich and the poor can be miserly and both can be generous. Tight-fistedness is the inverse of large heartedness. It is not about lack of money. That said, the problem of miserliness appears to have two faces. Subjectively, the miser is saddled with terrible anxiety; parting with money stirs up in him the dread of becoming poor and resourceless. Saving money is equated with psychic security and the slightest monetary bleed is felt to be a life-threatening hemorrhage. The miser resorts to all sorts of conscious and unconscious measures to avoid spending. Rationalization especially comes to his rescue; it helps stinginess to masquerade as prudence. Inner tension nonetheless persists.

In contrast to such an anxiety-laden inner world, the miser's object relations are permeated with sadism, even though he is consciously unaware of it. His lack of generosity, his frequent cheating and unfairness in paying his due, becomes a torture to his friends and relatives. The miser seems to be saying to them: 'Why should I give you anything when I myself have not been given much?' This brings up the fact that while anal drive derivatives are clearly discernible in it (Freud, 1908; Jones, 1918), 'monetary constipation' is, at its bottom (pun unintended), a reaction to early oral deprivation. The miser has experienced a profound and traumatizing lack of nourishment from his early caretakers and, in a move typical of 'identification with the aggressor' (A. Freud, 1936), has adapted an ungiving attitude towards others. Yesterday's victim has become today's perpetrator. The miser's self is split; a deprived child weeps inside while a cruel and withholding adult triumphantly parades outside.

Characterological Overspending

Many individuals resort to spending sprees in states of anxiety. Shopping serves as a distraction from inner turmoil and the act of buying becomes a reassurance against passivity and ego-impotence (Benson, 2000). Feelings of inferiority are masked by flashes of financial omnipotence. Depressive affects can also be warded-off.[19]

Besides such 'state-related' financial excesses, there are patterns of overspending that are better viewed as 'trait-related'. Highly repressed, neurotic individuals over-spend money to derive sexual gratification in disguise.

> The spending of money deceives them as to the want of freedom of their libido and thus relieves them for a short time of the painful feeling of sexual insufficiency. In other words, they are under an abnormally strict

prohibition, proceeding from the parental imago, against expending their libido freely. A compromise between instinct and repression is made by which the patient, in a spirit of defiance, does expend—not his sexual libido but an anal currency. (Abraham, 1917, p. 301)

The motives for overspending in individuals with narcissistic, hypomanic, and antisocial personalities (Akhtar, 1992) are different. They like to throw lavish parties, give huge tips, buy costly dresses, drive flashy cars, and go on exorbitantly expensive trips. All this is often accompanied by a pretended contempt for money in real life (Jones, 1913). The motivations underlying such behavior include self-aggrandization, defying the limits of resources, dazzling others, buying gratitude, and drawing secondary gains from making an impression. Money becomes an instrument of 'manic defense' (Klein, 1935; Winnicott, 1935).

Inordinate Generosity

In contrast to the exhibitionistic and self-indulgent overspending of money described above, the syndrome of 'inordinate generosity' involves giving excessive amounts of money to others. Such behavior is distinct from genuine philanthropy where a resourceful individual donates money for civic causes. In situations of 'inordinate generosity', the individual often does not have much money himself and the recipient is not needy in reality, only construed as such in the giver's mind. The dynamics of this undue financial indulgence in others is the same as seen in 'pseudo altruism' where

> compulsive caretaking and self-sacrifice cloaks and defends against aggression, envy, and a need to control the object. There is generally little or no conscious pleasure in the behavior, although the analytic observer can detect evidence of sadistic glee in the dramatic exhibitions of suffering that aim, generally unconsciously, at coercing others. (Seelig & Rosof, 2000, p. 948)

Monetary Masochism

This is evident in individuals who display some or all of the following behaviors (i) not asking for a salary raise even when they are deserving of it, (ii) turning down opportunities for making more money, (iii) chronically asking lower than market price for their services, (iv) not being able to spend money on their own selves, (v) not investing their capital in ways that assure its maximal growth, (vi) being unable to firmly conduct financial negotiations, (vii) frequently misplacing and losing money, (viii) not being able to use or enjoy expensive gifts given to them, and (ix) becoming depressed or self-injurious, however subtly, upon receiving a windfall. Such 'monetary masochism' occupies an intermediate place between 'moral' and 'erotic' (Freud, 1924) varieties of masochism insofar as it is highly libidinized, can result in physical suffering, but does not involve overt sexual enactment. The 'beating fantasy' (A. Freud, 1922) typical of erotic masochism lurks just beneath the surface and the 'pleasure' in financial hardship is discernible to the experienced eye.

Bargain Hunting

The tendency shown by some individuals to be irresistibly attracted to merchandise that they do not need but can buy cheaply constitutes the essence of 'bargain hunting'. The object's price is more important here than its usefulness. In Bergler's (1947) words,

> The act of buying is for the bargain hunter not a rational situation but a battle of wits. He tries to outsmart the seller, who, on the other hand, seeks to give him, the involuntary 'sucker', the narcissistic illusion of triumph... bargain hunters behave as if bad reality (mother substitute) wants to refuse and must be outsmarted with aggression which shows up in the tenacity of the bargaining process. (p. 625)

The pleasure of victory experienced by the bargain hunter is, however, short-lived. It is soon replaced by 'buyer's remorse' and doubt about the 'success' of the transaction. 'Could I have gotten the stuff for even less?' the bargain hunter wonders. This anguish is the masochistic counterpart of his oral sadism which fuels his greed.

Pathological Gambling

Closely related to 'bargain hunting' is the syndrome of pathological gambling. Here the wish to get something cheap reaches its zenith. The disproportion between the amount spent (e.g., on lottery tickets, roulette, off-track betting) and the desired reward (in thousands and millions of dollars) creates the illusion that what one is about to receive is free of charge. This constitutes a powerful allure since it secretly gratifies the infantile wish of getting something for nothing. After all, it is only in infancy and childhood that one actually gets free supplies (tangible or emotional); once that period of life has passed, all material acquisition and even all love and respect has to be earned. Gambling, by 'promising' a windfall and a generous gift from the 'mother nature', as it were, creates the possibility of being a carefree child again. At the same time, ignoring the fact that the probability of winning is minuscule (a fact that *is* preconsciously known), prepares the ground for masochistic self-punishment; the guilt over resorting to an unfair and effortless path to success (unconsciously equated with transgression of the oedipal barrier which demands respect for generational boundaries and therefore of time) is thus relieved.[20]

Addiction to gambling has a special connection with masturbation. Both involve arousal, excitement, and climax. Both deploy punishment for the activity per se as a plea bargain for keeping the fantasies involved in them unconscious. And, both are intended as a sort of play.

> Masturbation in childhood and puberty, in this sense, is 'playing at' sexual excitement, acquainting the ego with this excitement, and preparing it for the ability to control it. Gambling, in the beginning, is also thought of as 'playing' in the sense that the 'oracle' is playfully asked how it would decide in a more serious situation. Under the pressure of inner tensions, the playful character may be lost; the ego can no longer control what is has initiated, but is overwhelmed by a very serious vicious cycle of anxiety, violent need for reassur-

ance, and anxiety about the intensity of this violence. The pastime becomes a matter of life and death. (Fenichel, 1945, p. 373)

Having surveyed the various symbolic functions of money and having briefly gone over the various psychopathological syndromes involving it, we are now prepared to plunge into the discourse about the impact of money upon the practice of psychotherapy and psychoanalysis.

SETTING FEES, BILLING AND THIRD-PARTY INVOLVEMENT

Setting of fees constitutes an important step in beginning the patient's treatment. On the one hand, it establishes, beyond doubt, that the therapist-patient relationship is a professional one. On the other hand, the very act of setting fees can reveal hitherto hidden information about the patient's inner dynamics and actual life circumstances. It is therefore surprising to note that the coverage of this issue differs greatly in books on psychotherapy. Some (e.g. Colby, 1951) do not mention it at all. Others (e.g. Menninger & Holzman, 1973) go over it briefly, using a rather authoritarian tone where the patient is told what to do rather than being made a partner in such decisions. Then there are books (Bruch, 1974; Roth, 1987; Ursano, Sonnenberg & Lazar, 1998) that address the matter in a thoughtful manner, emphasizing the need for candid and thorough discussion of the fee, insurance payments, charging for missed sessions, and, above all, the patient's freedom to decline to participate in the financial arrangements proposed by the therapist and seek help elsewhere.

It is, however, Jacobs (1986) who provides the most lucid and thoughtful discussion of setting fees for psychotherapy. Prominent among the points he makes are the following:

• The amount to be charged for each session should be explicitly discussed between the therapist and patient during the initial evaluation. Such discussion might have to include an exploration of the patient's assets and income from various sources.

- Since dynamic psychotherapy and psychoanalysis are long-term endeavors, the sustained nature of the patient's financial resources should be assessed. Contingency plans in case of the patient's resources drying up should also be addressed at this early stage. Leaving them for later is hardly prudent since at that stage issues of transference and countertransference are likely to muddle the clinical picture.

- The therapist should mention his 'usual' fee only if he is going to stick to that very figure or make only minimal reductions to it. Telling a patient one's 'usual fee' and then accepting a significantly lower amount can puzzle the patient; both narcissistic fantasies of being 'special' to the therapist and a guilty sense of having unwittingly burdened him can arise as a consequence.

- There are exceptional instances where the therapist might deliberately agree to a lower fee than is realistically possible for the patient to pay. This is done for psychodynamic reasons since some (e.g. schizoid and depressed) individuals cannot otherwise be engaged in treatment. 'It is also true for certain patients who have subtle difficulties with ego boundaries and for whom paying less assures them of a comfortable separateness which they may need in order to enter an intensive treatment' (Jacobs, 1986, p. 127). Eissler (1949) had made the same point, long ago, in connection with mildly antisocial individuals.

To these sensible recommendations, I will only add that the fee, regardless of its actual amount, must be realistic for the circumstances of both the patient and therapist. If the patient, for some reason, agrees to pay a higher fee than he can afford, he will sooner or later begin to resent the treatment; this, in turn, will contribute to his resistances. If the patient manages to have his therapist accept a fee that is less than what he can actually afford, he will sooner or later begin to feel guilty; this will cause problems for their work. The same dual dynamics applies to the therapist. If he charges the patient an inordinately high fee, he is prone to feel guilty just as if he accepts a very low fee, he is likely to feel resentment. The lesson from all this is crystal clear: the fee must be realistic for both parties. And, if their realities cannot match without gross adjustments, the advisability of their working together becomes questionable.[21]

A few other points are important here. First, therapists are accustomed to exploring a patient's declaration that he cannot afford to pay their fee but take another patient's agreement to pay the demanded fee at surface value. Such an attitude overlooks that a quick agreement on the patient's part might be unrealistic. Interview-related anxiety and characterological timidity might cloud the patient's judgment in this regard. Cultural factors might also pay a role here. Negotiations of fee with recent immigrants from Far Eastern countries, for instance, must take into account that their socially-dictated reverence for authority might be making it difficult for them to ask for a lesser and more realistic fee.[22]

The second issue pertains to the frequency of payments. Most therapists bill on a monthly basis but there are some who wish to be paid at each session. This might be financially prudent but it is psychologically insensitive. It carries the potential of conveying that the therapist does not trust the patient or that he is unduly anxious about money matters. Such repeated reminders of the business aspect of the relationship deprive the patient of the much-needed illusion of unconditional acceptance in the setting of which transference can develop and internal objects become mobilized. Moreover, the patient who pays at each session is prone to assess the value of an individual hour separately rather than that of the therapy as an on-going process.

Finally, there is the impact of third-party payers on setting and collecting of fees. Ideally, this variable would not exist. But it does and has to be dealt with. The potential breach of confidentiality, while unavoidable to a certain extent, must be kept to a minimum (Chodoff, 1986; Ursano et al., 1998). In general, the therapist should be available to provide a bill in the format required by the patient's insurance company and/or be willing to sign the needed forms. The current climate of practice, with its provider networks, often makes it necessary to accept insurance payments directly and receive only the 'co-payments' from the patient. However, if there is a choice, it is preferable that the patient be responsible to deal with and submit the bill to the insurance company; this keeps the financial dialogue and its attendant affects and fantasies contained within the therapeutic dyad.

The same policy (i.e. of assuring that the patient deals with the 'third parties'), by and large, applies to very young adults (e.g. college students) whose treatment is being paid for by their parents.[23]

CLINICAL VIGNETTE 10

Erin Nevin, a twenty year-old college student sought psychotherapy for depression that was making it difficult for her to do the required academic work. During the initial evaluation, she told her psychiatrist that her parents, who owned a highly successful restaurant in a large mid-western city, would pay for her treatment; all he had to do was send them a monthly bill. The psychiatrist declined saying: 'Look, you are an adult, a young adult but nonetheless an adult, and you have to be responsible for paying your bill. Where you get the money is up to you but I will only accept payment from you.' Erin protested saying that the psychiatrist she had previously seen had accepted such an arrangement. Undaunted by Erin's argument, her psychiatrist refused to bill her parents. He felt that doing so would be harmful in two ways: (i) it would make Erin feel as if her treatment was being carried on free of charge and thus fuel a sense of infantile omnipotence in her, and (ii) it would preclude her realizing that her parents were indeed spending hard-earned money on her treatment.

On rare occasions, however, this policy can be reversed if the decision to do so is based on solid psychodynamic reasons. For instance, an older woman analyst seeing a young out-of-town college freshman, who has never felt loved by his mother, might accept to receive payments directly from his parents. She would be doing this in order to provide her patient the much-needed illusion of unconditional love as a preliminary condition for beginning treatment, knowing fully well that sooner or later this would have to become a topic for exploration and understanding.

CHARGING FOR MISSED SESSIONS

Psychodynamic psychotherapy or psychoanalysis requires that the patient come two to five times per week for sessions with his therapist. This needs discipline. While pre-arranged absences that have been realistically discussed and interpretively explored cause less disturbance to the flow of the therapeutic process, it is the unexpected, sudden, and impulsive absence from the session that draws greater analytic attention. Purposes of resistance, acting-out, and transference-based enactments can all be served by such 'missed sessions'. Clearly all this has to be analytically handled— i.e. by confrontation, exploration, interpretation, and reconstruction. However, the aspect that becomes quite 'charged' (pun intended) for the novice is whether to bill the patient for a missed session or not.

In one of his technique papers, Freud (1913) emphasized that the patient 'rents' hours from the therapist and is responsible for paying even if he does not make use of them. This gradually became the standard practice, or at least the practice that has been customarily upheld as desirable. Ursano et al. (1998) have eloquently explicated the rationale for this technical stance, regarding it to be

> the most neutral and fundamentally respectful stance
> for the therapist to take. Otherwise, the therapist takes
> the position of making a moral judgment about
> whether the absence was justified. In such a case, the
> therapist, in effect, volunteers to make a personal fi-
> nancial sacrifice if an absence is deemed worthy of be-
> ing excused. If the patient is angered by paying for a
> missed hour, there is then an opportunity to explore
> the dynamics of the anger and why the patient feels
> that the therapist should absorb the exigencies of the
> patient's life. Similarly, the therapist operating on
> these guidelines can more appropriately set fees re-
> flecting a known stability of chargeable hours and
> therefore potentially lower per-session fee. (p. 174)

To me, these 'explanations' and the value system that underlies them appear harsh, self-serving, and devoid of physicianly kindness. I assert the following: (i) Freud's recommendations were developed nearly a hundred years ago when life's pace was slower, analyses were shorter, and authoritarian models of clinical work prevailed. Those recommendations may have little applicability to the changed social and clinical milieu of today. (ii) Freud was a private practitioner with a large number of dependents and no other source of income beside clinical practice; his policy of charging for missed sessions reflected his personal situation and is less relevant to those practicing under different circumstances. (iii) While psychotherapy and psychoanalysis do require a certain asymmetry (with the patient revealing his inner world and the therapist withholding personal information), this asymmetry does not extend to all aspects of their work. Since the 'exigencies' of the therapist's life (e.g. illness, pregnancy, professional meetings) can and do impact upon the patient, it is morally unfair not to have the therapeutic frame accommodate the 'exigencies' of the patient's life. (iv) The assumption that the anger felt by the patient at being charged for a missed session is something that needs 'exploration' is also open to question. It blocks the consideration that the patient's anger at this situation might, at times, be legitimate.[24]

Clearly, there is a dialectical tension between the two positions outlined above; indeed, they represent one particular derivative of what Strenger (1989) has broadly termed the 'classic' and 'romantic' visions of psychoanalysis. The two approaches view human life differently, embody different ethical values, and give rise to different therapeutic strategies. A rigid clinging to either extreme is not useful even though it might provide the comfort of having clear-cut guidelines regarding clinical work. The fact is that most clinicians somehow end up striking a balance between these extremes and this applies to their policy of charging or not charging for missed sessions as well.

Four situations that might suggest not charging include absences due to: (i) developmentally appropriate out-of-town interludes (for visiting parents, study abroad) of college students; (ii) serious medical illness of the patient, and, according to Pasternak (1986) of the patient's immediate family members; (iii) family vacations which the patient, despite earnest effort, could not manage to match with the therapist's time away; and (iv) natural disasters.[25] This recommendation might invite the criticism of the purists that the therapist is taking a superego position and flaunting moral authority. A rejoinder to this would be that the therapist is actually taking an ego position and showing respect for reality. And, in all fairness, it should be acknowledged that even these four situations can be used for the purposes of resistance and enactment. The recommendation of making an allowance for them is therefore relative and not absolute. While the novice might benefit by erring on the side of caution, with experience one learns that, when all is said and done, charging or not charging is all a matter of tact, empathic attunement, common sense, and analytic understanding of the situation. A far cry from water-tight policies, this stance reminds one of Limentani's (1989) solemn observation that 'psychoanalysis is an art and for this reason it needs discipline' (p. 260).

MONEY, TRANSFERENCE AND COUNTERTRANSFERENCE

The deployment of a monetary idiom in the service of repressed and unresolved infantile desires is far from uncommon. Stated in simpler terms, this means that money is frequently used by patients to express and enact transference wishes (and defenses against them) involving the therapist. A frequent manifestation of this is withholding payments or inordinately delaying them. The therapist, faced with this problem, has to decipher whether it is a characterological pattern or a specific development in the transference. The former might need more active confrontation and limit-setting while the latter needs to be handled in the more customary fashion of interpretation.

A related situation is when the patient loses a job or encounters a financial setback. Regardless of the extent to which such a mishap can be psychodynamically understood, the therapist is faced with a dilemma: terminate the treatment and refer the patient to a low-fee clinic or keep seeing him while extending credit to him in the form of deferred payments. A number of variables come into play here. These include: (i) the therapist's degree of comfort with his own financial situation, (ii) the overall value system of the therapist, especially as it involves matters of money, neediness, dependence, generosity, and so on, (iii) the nature of the financial emergency, especially whether it can be realistically assessed as transient or protracted, (iv) the patient's erstwhile reliability both as an individual and a partner in the therapeutic dyad, (v) the availability of reasonably good low-fee care, (vi) the current state of transference and countertransference, and so on. A complex grid of variables thus guides decision-making for the therapist encountering such a situation. In general, unpaid bills should not be allowed to accrue for a long time and any extension of 'credit' to the patient should be short-term. Collecting interest on delayed bills, however rationally justifiable it may be, seems unkind, contrary to the generative attitude that is integral to being a therapist, and therefore might turn out to be anti-therapeutic. Of course, if the patient feels guilty at not paying interest, his inability to tolerate gratitude can become a topic for exploration.

Yet another manifestation of 'monetary transference' is the patient's spontaneous offer to increase the fee, for instance, in an attempt to 'seduce' the analyst away from potentially painful introspective work, while remaining oblivious to his unconscious intent.

Clinical Vignette 11

Dr. Robert Purple sought help when he found himself falling in love with 'yet another inappropriate woman'. A forty year-old internist with a mildly apologetic but earnest and decent way of relating, Dr. Purple had been twice divorced, both times having 'discovered' that he had married far beneath his socioeconomic and intellectual status. The current situation was different only on the surface; the inappropriateness of the choice became readily evident with questioning during the initial assessment.

Dr. Purple had grown up with a father who was preoccupied with his work and a mother who was anxious and clinging to her two sons. Dr. Purple's older brother had been difficult from childhood onwards; local police were often knocking at their otherwise respectable door. Assuming a quiet and passive stance, Dr. Purple grew up to be a kind and industrious man who somehow never blossomed fully, either as a professional or as a lover. He accepted a humdrum job and twice married needy and impaired women.

Soon after beginning treatment with me, he offered to raise the amount he was paying me. Since little evidence could be unearthed that he had misrepresented his financial status at the time when we decided the fee, and had not received a salary raise, I was intrigued by this offer. My encouragement for him to elaborate on this idea gradually revealed that he viewed me as an immigrant physician with few well-paying patients; he wanted to help me. I was going to be his next rescue project, it seemed. A transferential re-creation of his needy mother (made more rescue-worthy by the condensation of a realistic perception of her character with the primal scene fantasies of her being beaten by the father) was essentially the motivating force behind Dr. Purple's gesture.

A more dramatic example of such transference-based 'generosity' is provided by Rothstein (1986) who describes a patient's offer to donate a huge sum of money in order to establish a research foundation bearing both their names. Exploration of this wish revealed the desire to remain united with the therapist (to undo the traumatic separation from his mother during childhood). Giving money to the therapist also assured his loyalty and helped bypass the analysis of the mistrust that the therapist would not really be there for him when he needed love and support. Money was to serve as glue between them.

In contrast to such direct allusions to money are situations where the patient strenuously avoids mentioning money when this would appear logically expectable.

Clinical Vignette 12

Paul Marcus, a recently married and highly competitive mid-level administrator, was in the process of buying a house while in intensive treatment with me. There were many determinants of this decision and all sorts of fantasies were stirred up by the houses he and his wife saw in the process. Things began to calm down once they settled on a particular house and made a formal offer. Paul would now talk enthusiastically about this house, describing its pros and cons in painstaking detail. While the transference wish that I be impressed by his thoughtfulness was evident, it struck me as more significant that he never mentioned the price of his forthcoming purchase. I brought this to his attention. He responded by acknowledging that this was difficult for him to do. As we explored further, it turned out that he was worried that I might mock him upon hearing the price of the house since I must own a house that was much more expensive. Empathizing with him, I nonetheless encouraged him to elaborate further. Now a second fantasy emerged: what if his house was more expensive than mine? Would that not be a 'crushing blow' to me? Looking at these two scenarios, it became clear that the price of this house was no longer a matter of external reality; it had become caught up in his hostile competitiveness with me (and, behind that, with his father whom he deeply loved, hated, and feared). By not mentioning the price of the house, Paul could keep these difficult feelings out of our exploratory work.

Yet another manifestation of money's involvement in transference-based anxieties is evident in the following vignette lent to me by a female colleague.

CLINICAL VIGNETTE 13

In the second year of Charlie Kim's analytic treatment, the first explicit exploration of erotic feelings came up. It was when—noting his 'erect' manner of entering my office, associations to fleeting incestuous thoughts about his sister, and his lively flirtation with one of my female patients in the waiting room—I decided gently to unmask the potential transference reference in all this. I said: 'I wonder if you ever find yourself struggling with similar erotic feelings in here, with me.' He responded by saying: 'I have thought about you, yes, I have. This is so hard to say. This is one of the most difficult things to talk about. I have looked at your boobs a few times, coming in. I can't believe I said that... I have these passing thoughts and fantasies... you probably think I am a horn dog... All these feelings are disgusting.'

As he went on and on, oscillating between sexual confessions and guilt-ridden self-admonishments, I noticed that he made no reference to any potential erotic competitors of his vis-à-vis me. When, in a later session, I pointed this out, he responded with the following: 'I try not to think about your husband... He is probably some good looking, muscular, rich guy. One of these types, who makes four-five hundred thousand dollars a year. See, that's why I never think of him. I avoid it. Yet I have to admit that he has crossed my mind a few times. I would never bring him up though. I could never compare to him. I feel like a total loser. I could never compete with him.' It was clear that Charlie defended against oedipal competition by undue self-diminishment and a neurotic over-exaltation of his rival's prowess. He made it appear that the competition was over before it began. Charlie's estimation of my husband's income was an example of 'denial by exaggeration' (Fenichel, 1945); he put my husband so out of competitive reach that he did not have to bring his hostile feeling towards him out into the open for analytic exploration. Big money served as a shield against phallic competition (and the associative dread of defeat) in the oedipal transference.

Clearly, concerns and fantasies involving money can be used for expressing a variety of transference wishes (e.g. seductive, hostile) and equally varied defenses against them. However, this should not lead one to overlook that matters of money impact upon the therapist's subjectivity as well.

Being human, the therapist brings his own feelings, fantasies, desires, and values regarding money to the clinical situation. The more financially stressed he is and the more his total income depends upon direct clinical work, the greater is his vulnerability to countertransference difficulties in this realm. Such current stressors, at times, come into tantalizing but painful play with the therapist's characterological soft spots (e.g. greed, masochism) on the one hand and the patient's monetary 'seductions' and 'tortures' on the other. Charging different fees to different patients also exposes the therapist to potential countertransference pitfalls. An even greater tendency for the countertransference to become problematic is evident in the treatment of the very wealthy and the very poor.

TREATING PHENOMENALLY WEALTHY PATIENTS

Working with phenomenally wealthy patients poses special challenges. To begin with, such patients, and especially their children, bring along with them an attitude of entitlement. Used to having their wishes and whims quickly gratified, they might find the plodding work of psychotherapy too slow and boring. Their 'superego lacunae' (Szurek & Johnson, 1953) might facilitate the sequestering of impulse-ridden sectors of personality; this might impede the integrative and probing efforts of the therapist.

Even in the absence of such difficulties, there is a great risk of countertransference problems in the treatment of wealthy patients. Feeling 'proud' to have a rich individual in treatment, gossiping about the patient's finances, envy of the patient, defensive contempt, undue deference and, born out of this, a tendency to avoid embarrassing material or excessively to accommodate schedule changes are among the major manifestations of countertransference-based impediment of treatment (Stone, 1972; Wahl, 1974; Olsson, 1986). The risk of such developments increases if the 'state' and/or 'trait' related vulnerabilities of the therapist are painfully stirred up by his wealthy patient's talk of money.

CLINICAL VIGNETTE 14

Pamela Kasinetz, an elderly woman with extreme wealth, sought psychotherapy for depression and anxiety of recent origin. The apparent trigger for this was the worsening relationship with her husband of over three decades. With their children no longer at home, the two had become quite alienated; he was engrossed in his business and she with her social commitments and philanthropic work. Matters became worse when Pamela ran into an 'adorable' seven or eight year-old Cambodian boy in a shopping mall and 'fell in love with him'. She took it upon herself to help him and his financially strained family. The boy gradually became her constant companion. Paying huge sums of money to his parents, Pamela pretty much took over his life. She would pick him up from school, bring him home, shower him with lavish gifts, and indulge all his whims and desires; his friends also were welcome at her house and were treated with similar indulgence. While numerous examples can be given, one instance should suffice, where she spent in excess of thirty thousand dollars over a weekend entertaining her little 'friend' and his four playmates. All this led to frequent arguments between Pamela and her husband who insisted on putting limits on her expenses.

Seeking symptomatic relief, Pamela appeared unprepared to look into the deeper meanings of her fascination with this little boy. Raised in a family of means, she readily dismissed any inquiry into a childhood sense of feeling deprived and thus blocked the therapist's efforts at linking her runaway altruism with potential unconscious issues pertaining to early trauma. It was all 'real' and rationalized in terms of kindness and generosity towards the underprivileged, as far as she was concerned. Soon after starting treatment, she expressed a desire to pay a much greater fee for her sessions, quoting what appeared to be truly an exorbitant amount. The situation was complicated by parallel problems in the therapist's countertransference to her and to the financial glitter of the situation. Having suffered a childhood parental loss at about the same age as the Cambodian boy Pamela so adored, and being financially strapped himself owing to a recent personal crisis, the therapist was made terribly uncomfortable by Pamela's financial seductions. Reacting defensively, he not only made premature trans-

ference interpretations but also sternly rejected her offers. He failed to explicate and explore them in a
peaceful manner. Pamela soon dropped out of treatment.

This adverse outcome seems to have been the result of a number of factors in the therapist: (i) current financial distress made it
hard for him to listen peacefully to his patient's extravagance; it
stirred up too much greed, (ii) childhood trauma made it difficult
for him to hear about his patient's indulgence in a little boy; it
stirred up too much envy; and (iii) not seeking a consultation in
what was obviously a difficult clinical situation for him, it led to
defensive recoil and over-interpretation. Flying solo under these
circumstances was an inappropriate clinical choice. And yet, the vignette has didactic value. It reveals some important variables in
pre-empting, precluding, or gainfully using these emergent countertransference feelings, including the therapist's: (i) inner 'good
objects' (Klein, 1935; 1940), the presence of which will diminish his
vulnerability to greed and envy, (ii) aptitude and skill for learning
from his subjective experiences in the course of treatment and (iii)
willingness to seek outside consultation in difficult clinical situations.

TREATING INDIGENT PATIENTS AND WORKING GRATIS

Difficulties also arise in working with the poor. Their lives are at
the mercy of socio-economic forces and their subjective experience
is often riddled with a sense of marginality, helplessness, and resig-
nation. Often the families they originate from are broken beyond
repair; there is deprivation of both maternal care and paternal
guidance. Lacking hope to escape their economic entrapment, such
individuals lack impulse control and become action-prone; Boris'
(1976) notion that hope and desire are inversely related is pertinent
in this context.[26] They seek dynamic psychotherapy infrequently
and their preoccupation with the different realities of their lives
have a discouraging effect upon the psychotherapist. Indeed, it has
been declared by some (Ruiz, 1981; Sue & Sue, 1977) that dynamic
psychotherapy is irrelevant in the context of their lives.

At the same time, it is possible that a discouraged therapist is manifesting a class-related and value-based countertransference reaction which, in a circular fashion, adds to the patient's 'untreatability' by dynamic psychotherapy (Javier, 1996). Viewed from this perspective, the main issue to be examined is that of sociopolitical, aesthetic, and empathic fit between the patient and therapist. Conducting dynamic psychotherapy with the urban poor might indeed be possible if the therapist is willing to:

• Learn the language of the urban poor, not only in regard to its colloquialisms but its overall architecture of urgency, worry, and mistrust.

• Blend some educative measures that actively encourage verbal reformulation of symptoms and 'teach' the patient the importance of their personal dynamic history (Olarte & Lenze, 1984).

• Regard the patient's preoccupation with reality problems as legitimate material for elaboration without prematurely linking them with their potentially deeper meanings and usage.

• Titrate the degree to which 'affirmative interventions' (Killingmo, 1989) are mixed with interpretive work.

• Rely more upon the object-relations model than upon the ego-psychological model; the former permits viewing the patient's complaints about reality problems, pressuring the therapist for action, and frequently missing sessions as interactive and communicative phenomena and not merely intrapsychic events (Altman, 1993).

• Offer interpretations in the context of support rather than in the context of abstinence; in Pine's (1985) words this is 'striking when the iron is cold'.

The clinical flexibility of the therapist, however, must find a willing and able partner in the patient. Sometimes this turns out to be the case and other times not. At still other times, one comes across poor individuals who display considerable resilience, ego strength, and 'psychological mindedness' (see Chapter One) and can benefit from 'unaltered' dynamic psychotherapy and even psychoanalysis.[27]

Contrary to the prevalent notion that the patient must pay a fee for the treatment to be effective, there is evidence that those who cannot pay anything might also benefit from psychotherapy and psychoanalysis (Lorand & Console, 1958; Jacobs, 1986). A growing unease that the benefit of psychoanalytic treatment was available only to the affluent, and the awareness of the long history of philanthropy in medicine prompted Freud to declare in 1918 that sooner or later

> the conscience of the community will awake and admonish it that the poor man has just as much right to help for his mind as he now has to the surgeon's means of saving life; and that the neuroses menace the health of a people no less than tuberculosis, and can be left as little as the latter to the feeble handling of individuals. Then clinics and consultation-departments will be built, to which analytically trained physicians will be appointed, so that the men who would otherwise give way to drink, the women who have nearly succumbed under their burden of privations, the children for whom there is no choice but running wild or neurosis, may be made by analysis able to resist and able to do something in the world. This treatment will be free. (Quoted in Lorand & Console, 1958, p. 59)

Freud's vision led to the establishment of psychoanalytic clinics providing treatment at minimum or, at times, no fee at all.[28] At the same time, it was felt that gratis treatment might create difficulties. Among the expected problems were lessening of motivation, increased dependency, avoidance of negative transference, and countertransference resentment. Freud himself warned that 'gratuitous treatment enormously increases the transference relationship for young women, or the opposition to obligatory gratitude in young men arising from the father complex which is one of the most troublesome obstacles to treatment' (quoted in Lorand & Console, 1958, p. 60). However, he acknowledged that in many patients 'unpaid treatment led to excellent results without exciting any of these difficulties' (p. 60).

Putting all this together, it seems that if properly handled, gratis treatment can work as efficiently as one with fee. However, the following conditions must be met for such work to take root and proceed meaningfully.

- The financial situation of the patient must be explicitly and 'shamelessly' evaluated before the decision for gratis work is taken.

- Gratis work should not be undertaken by therapists who are themselves struggling with finances.

- Even those who have financial security should not take more than one or two patients on a pro bono basis.

- An attitude of flexibility must be maintained and fees should be introduced if the patient's reality changes.

The fact is that careful investigation almost invariably reveals that the patient can pay at least a small, token fee. The amount of that fee is significant for the patient even if it appears 'low' by all external standards; the patient should not be forcibly turned into a gratis patient and the 'low' fee should be regarded as reasonable.[29] This changes the ambiance of the clinical dyad. Of course the emotional meanings of being treated for a 'low' fee will have to be explored and understood in the course of treatment, especially if direct or disguised associations to it crop up in the clinical material.

Distinct from ongoing treatment done without fee, is the issue of offering one or two session-long consultations gratis. This practice is not infrequent though it is hardly discussed in the professional literature. For many therapists, this is simply a part of therapeutic 'good manners'. They do not charge fees for the initial consultation to patients referred by friends and acquaintances. Others extend a similar courtesy to junior colleagues in the mental health profession and other sundry categories of patients they select on various personal and professional grounds.[30] How many of these gratis consultations turn into ongoing treatments and to what extent the patient's retrospective feelings about those free sessions affect the course of therapy remains unknown. In my own experience, little negative impact of this initial indulgence is evident. In fact, it might add to a strengthening of the therapeutic alliance that evolves later on, even though the consultation is not done gratis for that reason.

REFUSING TO TAKE MONEY FROM PATIENTS

In contrast to clinical work done on a pro-bono basis due to the patient's lack of resources, there are situations where the therapist might refuse to accept money from patients for ethical and psychodynamic reasons. The treatment of patients whose income is derived from illegal activities constitutes one such situation. To be sure, hardened criminals are not the psychotherapist's frequent clients. Yet sometimes members of the mafia, professional call-girls and prostitutes, and drug dealers and smugglers do end up seeking help. To accept payments from them poses moral dilemmas, only some of which can be solved by consulting a colleague, seeking supervision, or obtaining formal legal advice. Certainly most therapists would not accept money if they knew that it was earned by running a pedophilic torture ring or committing murder on contract. But what about white collar criminals? Are the crimes of those investment bankers who rob the pension funds of the elderly any less sinister? The point here is that, in the end, it might boil down to the therapist's personal morality and judgment.

Less flagrant situations can also pose challenges. For instance, a wealthy patient might offer a huge sum of money to recruit the therapist to provide care only to him and no one else.[31] This, of course, cannot be accepted. Even the milder forms of such perverse enactment have to be dealt with by firm limit-setting.

CLINICAL VIGNETTE 15

'Richard Lambert' called me three months after his Latin-American psychiatrist had moved back to his country of origin. He said that he was following up on the advice of his psychiatrist to see me. However, he would only come if I accepted three conditions: he would never tell me his actual name; no record of his visits were to be kept, and he would pay my top fee, cash, at each session, but this transaction must not be recorded in any form. I responded by saying that I could not accept these conditions for the same reason that I could not reject them. He was puzzled at my response and asked me to repeat it. I did so. He, unsatisfied, asked me if I were saying 'yes' or 'no' to his conditions. I told him that I was saying neither since I did not really know what all this was about and could not jump into actions in light of the fact that we had not even met and I knew nothing about him, his life, and his problems. I told him that if he could tolerate such ambiguity and maintain open-mindedness, then he would come and, if not, then he would go elsewhere. He thought for a while and then said that he would like to make an appointment.

Upon arriving in my office a few days later, 'Richard' did not sit down. Instead, he paced through my office, picking up books and commenting upon them, touching knick-knacks. Impeccably dressed, tall, and in his mid-fifties, he cut an impressive figure. Nonetheless, there was an eerie feeling to what was unfolding in front of my eyes. Attempts on my part to engage him in the customary gambits of initial assessment (see Chapter One) failed. He brushed them aside. He would neither tell me his name nor give me an address, phone number, or any identifying information. After this strange 'clinical' dance went on for nearly forty-five minutes, I called the meeting off. Upon this, he, still standing, took out a big wad of dollar bills from his pocket, and asked me how much he should pay me. I responded by saying: 'For what?' He said: 'For the time you spent with me. Shouldn't I be paying for it?' I said: 'No, I don't think so. It is true that I charge money for clinical work but what has transpired here does not qualify as that and therefore I cannot accept this money.' He was taken aback. After one or two repetitions of basically the same exchange between us, he left my office. I never heard from him again.

Accepting money from this 'patient' would have created a mis-alliance whereby I would have colluded in bringing upon a funda-mental distortion of the therapeutic frame. Psychotherapy cannot be practiced and must not be started under circumstances that defy reality, especially when repudiation of consensual truth is so outra-geous and violent as it was in this case.

Yet another instance where the therapist might refuse to accept money from the patient is when the offer is based upon a near-delusional idea and taking money conveys an agreement with such distorted thinking.

CLINICAL VIGNETTE 16

During her analytic treatment, Carol Dunson, a thirty-seven year-old unmarried attorney with pronounced depressive proclivities, would frequently be in the throes of a powerful negative transference. At such times, she would become convinced that her therapist despised her; she would feel intensely angry towards him. Empathic holding and transference interpreta-tion which linked her perception of the therapist to her feeling rejected by her mother in childhood would alleviate the affective tension for some time. Then she would become regressed again, losing the clarity she had just gained. The therapeutic work continued in a staccato fashion and then took a downward swing as Carol developed a disturbing physical ailment. Though causing considerable distress, the illness was not life-threatening. Carol, however, felt otherwise. She was convinced that the disease would kill her and, during a dip into her usual negative transference feelings, became nearly delusional in her conviction.

One day, she arrived at her therapist's office with two checks in hand. One was for the last month's fee that indeed was due. The other check was for the few sessions that she had had in the current month and for which the usual monthly bill was yet to be given to her. She offered the two checks to the therapist, ex-plaining that she did not want him to get stuck with unpaid bills for the current month since she was going to die within the next day or so. The therapist was taken aback at this 'earnest' offer but soon regained his composure. Declining to take the second check, he insisted that the sources of her certainty about her impending death should be explored. He also noted that his accepting the check would 'confirm' that he too believed that she was going to die; that the patient was unconsciously imploring him to show her that this was not so gradually became explicit as the session progressed.

To summarize, it seems that there are at least three circumstances in which the therapist might refuse to accept money from a patient: (i) when the source of money goes diametrically against the therapist's ethical standards, (ii) when accepting the money would be a collusion to form a perverse alliance, and (iii) when money is offered in the throes of an intense transference regression.

CONCLUDING REMARKS

In this chapter, I have discussed the emotional significance of money and attempted to show the ways in which it impacts upon the work of psychotherapy. The areas I have addressed range from symbolism and psychopathology through the setting of fees and charging (or not charging) for missed sessions to the myriad transference and countertransference reverberations of monetary exchange within the clinical dyad. I have also elucidated, albeit briefly, the special problems that emerge in the treatment of extremely wealthy and very poor and indigent patients. Finally, I have described some unusual situations where a firm refusal to accept money offered by a patient seems the only therapeutically and ethically right thing to do.

Throughout this discourse, I have paid attention to the fact that what we encounter as clinical phenomena are the end products of a complex interplay between reality and fantasy, between the wild lyricism of id and stern admonishments of superego, between spontaneity and falsehood, and, above all, between transference and countertransference exchanges. Locating them in this ever-shifting complexity does rob one of the opportunity to make up 'rules' that would be correct for all circumstances. It forces one to take a pause, think, reflect upon prior knowledge and experience, read some more, and, if still unclear, seek some supervision or collegial input. It nudges the therapist towards humility. The clinical situation that forms the topic of my next chapter can put the need for such humility to its utmost test.

4. Disruptions

Things never do go smoothly in suicides, weddings, and courtships.

Mark Twain (1835-1910)

In an aphoristic statement, the quintessentially American psycho-analyst, Harry Stack Sullivan, is known to have said: 'Beware of smoothly going therapy'. At one level, we all attest to the wisdom of this statement. At another level, however, we continue to hold on to the idea that psychotherapeutic endeavors could or should go on without a hitch. Clinical experience shows us otherwise. Our patients 'disappoint' us. They walk out, act out, and drop out, leaving us baffled, embarrassed or even resentful.

Keeping this in mind, it seems imperative that we attempt to understand what such 'disruptions' mean, how they arise, what their dynamics are, and how they can be mended. Other questions also need to be faced. Are all disruptions, for instance, 'bad'? Do disruptions happen in the course of all psychotherapies or only in the treatment of patients with severe character pathology? Are disruptions avoidable? Are there developmental prototypes for disruptions? In other words, are there normative aspects to the disruptions of dialogue between a patient and his or her therapist? And, finally, can disruptions ever be an indication that the treatment is progressing well?

The search for preliminary answers to these questions forms the impetus of this chapter. In it, I will (i) offer a definition of the concept of 'disruption', (ii) bring together the models of its etiology

99

that seem scattered throughout psychoanalytic literature, (iii) describe various manifestations of disruptions with the help of brief clinical vignettes, (iv) discuss the technical dilemmas in dealing with these difficult clinical situations, and (v) seek to anchor my recommendations in some child-development observations.

What Constitutes A 'Disruption'?

The term 'disruption has no 'official' definition. It does not appear in psychiatric (Hinsie & Campell, 1970) or psychoanalytic (Eidelberg, 1968; Rycroft, 1972; Moore & Fine, 1968, 1990; Laplanche & Pontalis, 1988) glossaries. More significantly, the term 'disruption' is not listed in the indices of the four most well-respected books on borderline conditions (Grinker et al., 1977; Gunderson, 1985; Kernberg, 1975; Stone, 1990). And yet, as a commonsense phrase, the expression 'disruption' is a daily guest in the chamber of clinical discourse. It is used loosely for interruptions of treatment due to reality reasons (e.g. money, relocation, finishing college) as well as for miscarriages of dialogue due to psychological reasons within the therapeutic dyad.

To bring some order to this laxity, I suggest that we restrict the use of the term to the latter situations. Defined in this way, a 'disruption' would have occurred when there is a (i) rupture of communication within the therapeutic dyad, (ii) sudden divergence in the agendas of the two parties, and (iii) threat to the safety or continuity of their ongoing work. This operational definition can, in some ways, be taken as a mirror-image of what are regarded to be the ingredients of a 'working' (Greenson, 1965), 'therapeutic' (Brenner, 1979), or 'helping' (Thomae & Kachele, 1994) alliance. With vantage points that vary only slightly, these three concepts refer to mutuality of purpose, agreement over methodology, and the pact of collaboration throughout the course of treatment, between the patient and the psychotherapist. Disruption is a serious impairment of such alliance between the two parties. A disruption can cause interruption of treatment. However, interruptions (especially those mutually agreed upon and developmentally or vocationally necessary) do not have to cause a disruption. Interruption is a factual matter. Disruption is a psychological event. Once we have arrived at this definition, we might begin looking for the underlying motivational factors that cause disruptions of the clinical dialogue.

UNDERLYING PSYCHODYNAMIC FACTORS

Within psychoanalytic literature, there seem to be many etiological models for the occurrence of a disruption. In the following passages, I offer a list of these models. However, in doing so, I am neither asserting one explanation's superiority over the other nor am I suggesting that some, owing to their being 'old', are less valid than others. I am also not suggesting that these models exist in an exclusive manner; more than one explanation usually applies to patients we see in clinical practice. Moreover, disruption is an interactional event and does not arise only from variables within the patient; the therapist might also contribute to the derailment of the clinical dialogue. It is with such caveats that the following models should be approached. Keeping them in mind would help the psychotherapist discern what might be going on at a deeper level with his or her patient.

Unconscious Guilt

Observing that certain patients got worse rather than better upon being understood in a correct fashion, Freud (1923) came up with the idea that an unconscious feeling of guilt was responsible for this unexpected disturbance. 'Negative therapeutic reactions' of this sort led the patient to become uncooperative, argumentative, and to manifest symptoms that had previously been resolved. They even impelled the patient to break off treatment. Freud speculated that a profound sense of unworthiness and a need for punishment existed under such disruptions of treatment. While he traced the source of such guilt to subterranean oedipal longings, the fact is that it could have emanated from other sources as well. For instance, individuals who have grown up around sickly siblings often carry unmet dependency needs and marked hostility arising out of such deprivation (Akhtar & Kramer, 1999). Inwardly remorseful about this hostility, they might find it difficult to enjoy the benefits of psychotherapy and disrupt its progress. The same applies to those who have lost their parents in their childhood. Such individuals suffer from 'survivor's guilt' (Niederland, 1981) which can propel them to disrupt their treatments.

Yet another group of individuals prone to guilt-driven disruptions are those in whom guilt was induced by parents during childhood. If, for instance, a mother makes it a point to repeatedly tell her offspring that her pregnancy and labor with him or her was very difficult and she almost lost her life in the process, then the child grows up feeling chronically guilty (Asch, 1976). Upon entering psychotherapy as an adult, he or she can hardly bear feeling understood and empathized with by the therapist. A tendency to disrupt treatment often accompanies such inner remorse.

Anxious Retreat From 'Higher' Level Conflicts

A second dynamics of disruptions involves the patient's regression due to the dread of facing newer intrapsychic conflicts once the intense, splitting-related issues are resolved. A borderline patient, for instance, struggles with incapacity to tolerate ambivalence. He idealizes people and, when they frustrate him, devalues them. No different in the clinical situation, he fluctuates between the extremes of adoring and hating the therapist. At both poles of his experience, matters appear simple and self-evident to him. Both transference configurations, however, lead to a cardboard-like image of the therapist in his mind. The patient seems incapable of containing the two representations simultaneously, combining them, developing a 'total' image, and refining it with tidbits of actual knowledge. Through the holding and containing functions of the therapist and with the use of 'bridging interventions'[32] (Kernberg, 1975; Akhtar, 1995, 1998), these capacities gradually arise. The patient begins to show a capacity for tolerating ambivalence and for genuinely knowing others. At this point, new anxieties crop up. It is like going from the frying pan to the fire. Usually pertaining to oedipal fantasies (with all their pressure of intrigue and pa, the patient once again becomes split, chaotic, and angst-ridden. The treatment ambiance, which had just become peaceful, becomes subject to chaos and acting out. Unable to bear exclusion from the real or imagined coupled life of the therapist

Sadomasochistic Need To Destroy A Helpful Situation

Patients with severe personality disorders often have suffered intense frustrations in childhood. Lack of love, chronic neglect, betrayal, physical and sexual abuse, and abandonment via desertion, divorce, or death often figure prominently in their developmental history (Akhtar, 1992, 1995). Such traumas fill them with pain, hurt, and hatred. As a result, when they enter treatment, they desperately want to be supported, praised, and loved. However, they also want to vent their pent-up anger and seek revenge from those who have hurt them (and the re-creations of such people in the transference). This inner pressure to attack caretakers becomes a powerful source of disruptions in their treatment (Kernberg, 1975).

A related dynamic emanates from the patient's envy of the therapist's capacity to remain calm and composed. The latter's ability to soothe and make helpful interventions stirs up the patient's envy. ('How can you make me feel better when I myself can not? What do you have that I lack?') This envy can propel attacks on the therapist and the therapeutic process (Klein, 1946). The life-enhancing function of seeing connections—between past and present, between love and hate, between childhood experiences and transference re-creations, and between the two parental figures—is also attacked. The result of such sadism, envy, 'attacks on linking' (Bion, 1959), and assaults on the healthy aspects of one's own mental functioning (since it is allied with the envy-producing therapist) is a serious disruption of clinical work.

Retreat Due To Separation Anxiety

Certain disruptions of treatment are caused by anxiety over having a separate existence of one's own. Narcissistically needy mothers who cannot let go of their children render them vulnerable to unconsciously equating separation with causing injury to them. Upon entering psychotherapy as adults, such 'children' experience any increase in distance (from their primary internal objects as well as from the transferential re-creations of them) as anxiety provoking. This, in turn, can cause them to regress and give up the gains derived from therapy. Modell (1965), Asch (1976) and Gruenert (1979) have described such negative therapeutic reactions based upon the anxiety of separation. I too have briefly commented elsewhere (Akhtar, 1991) on a patient who, with each progressive movement in her analysis, would develop a fear of abandonment by me and, motivated by this fear, regressively lose her laboriously acquired insights. In a related vein, Miller (1965) suggests that the exacerbation of symptoms during the terminal phase of analysis might also reflect a defense against separation anxiety.

Shift In Psychic Organization

It is conventional psychoanalytic wisdom that better-functioning patients are mostly organized around internal *conflicts* (e.g. 'What to do and what not to do?' 'What is the right course if I want to do what I should not do?') and those with severe personality disorders around internal *deficits* (e.g. 'How to be?' 'How to do this or that?'). However, in day-to-day practice, matters are more complex. All patients turn out to have areas of conflict and areas of deficit in their mental make-up. This is important to know since at the level of conflict, the patient is amenable to seeing hidden meanings in his or her communications. The patient also appears capable of waiting, listening, and cooperating with the therapist. However, when the patient hits an area of deficit, ego regression sets in (Balint, 1968; Killingmo, 1989). Words lose connotations. Language becomes simple. There develops a quality of monotonous repetition to the patient's demands. Leaving the terrain of 'contradiction' and 'paradox', the subjective experience enters the realm of 'simplicity' (Akhtar, 1998). If the therapist does not discern this change and shift his technique accordingly (see below), then he 'loses' contact with the patient. Their dialogue suffers and a disruption results.

Empathic Failures Of The Therapist

While the foregoing dynamics hints at the potential contribution of a therapist to clinical disruptions, more overt situations of iatrogenic impasses also exist. Some of these arise from the therapist's inexperience and the consequent technical rigidity. Others result from the therapist's failure of empathy (Kohut, 1977) or from specific countertransference lapses which make him lose touch with the patient's psychic reality. Under these circumstances:

> The patient feels misunderstood and unable to get through to the therapist. Perhaps the therapist seems more interested in himself and in his theories than the patient's concerns. Or, the therapist may seem to be more involved with the patient's family or other pre-

sumed adversaries than with the patient. Sometime the patient has the impression that the analyst is more interested in the patient's behavior than how he or she feels inside or that the analyst cares more about the analysand than who he or she is. (Wolf, 1993, p. 93)

As would be readily apparent, this sort of disruption has overlaps with the dynamics associated with shifting structural organization described above. The only difference is that here the therapist's contribution is largely emanating from within his or her psyche and is not a response to the altered situation within the patient's mind.

CLINICAL MANIFESTATIONS

The breakdown of communicative mutuality between the patient and therapist can be of varying degrees. Variables of duration, emotional intensity, threat to the framework of treatment, and risk of violence have to be taken into consideration here. The following clinical vignettes illustrate what can happen in such circumstances and how disruptions range from momentary ruptures of working alliance to broken therapeutic boundaries and threats of physical harm.

CLINICAL VIGNETTE 17

Judith Conahan, a highly intelligent lawyer with narcissistic personality disorder, was in analysis with me. For the first year or so, all she talked about was how she felt unloved by her husband and, during her childhood, by her mother. She never made a comment about me and in effect treated me with an indifference that was quite like she had received from her mother. Then, in the eighteenth month of her analysis, I announced that I had to take a few days off at rather short notice. The patient responded to the news with immediate acceptance and the usual lack of associations. The next day, however, she began her session by telling me that one of her clients had canceled an appointment that morning. During that hour, she went through her desk drawers and found her home insurance policy. Judith went on to tell me that she got quite upset upon reading parts of that policy. There were too many loopholes, too little coverage!

Discerning unmistakable allusions to my impending absence (e.g. 'canceled appointment', 'too little coverage') in her associations, I said: 'Perhaps, you find it easier to talk about an insurance policy with loopholes than an analysis with interruptions'. After a long pause, she responded in a pained voice: 'I can see how you arrived at what you said but it hurt my feelings because I was really worried about the policy and it seems that you are not paying attention to my concern about it.'

Here the 'disruption' that occurred was manifested by the long pause during which the patient obviously found it difficult to communicate with me. In quickly unmasking what lay behind a derivative of her feelings about our separation, I had overlooked the patient's need for disguise. I had disregarded her need to control the boundaries between her conscious and unconscious psychic life and to yield such control at her own pace. I had gone 'too deep' and my intervention had resulted in a 'micro-disruption'. Her communicating her distress to me showed that she had already bounced back from the momentary rupture of our dialogue. A more dramatic example of this is constituted by the following:

CLINICAL VIGNETTE 18

In the throes of a regressive transference, Patrice O'Malley entered my office enraged and waving a finger. Approaching the couch, she said: 'I have a lot on my mind today and I want to do all the talking. I don't want you to speak even a single word!' A little taken aback, I mumbled 'Okay.' Patrice shouted: 'I said "not a word" and you have already fucked up this session!' Now sitting on my chair behind her, I was more rattled. Did I do wrong by speaking at all? I asked myself. As she lay on the couch, angry and stiff, I started to think. Perhaps she is so inconsolable today, so intent upon forcing me into the role of a depriving

person, that she found a way to see even the gratification of her desire as its frustration. I was, however, not
entirely satisfied with this explanation and therefore
decided to wait, and think further. It then occurred to
me that maybe she was rightly angered by my saying
'Okay'. In my agreeing to let her have omnipotent
control over me, I had asserted my will and thus paradoxically deprived her of the omnipotence she
seemed to need. I was about to make an interpretation
along these lines, when it occurred to me that by shar-
ing this understanding, I would be repeating my mistake: making my autonomous psychic functioning too
obvious. As a result, I decided only to say, 'I am
sorry', and left the remaining thought unspoken.
Patrice relaxed and the tension in the room began to
lessen. After ten minutes of further silence, the patient
said, 'Well, this session has been messed up. I had so
many things to say.' After a further pause, she said:
'Among the various things on my mind...' and thus
the session gradually 'started'. By the time we ended,
things were going pretty smoothly.

In the first vignette, the disruption was mild and was mostly
caused by the inordinate depth and mistiming of my (content-wise,
correct) intervention. In the second vignette, the disruption was
more intense and was caused by an admixture of my natural and
friendly but dynamically misattuned remark and the patient's pre-
existing paranoid attitude. The contribution of the latter pole to
disruption dynamics is more clear in the following vignette.

CLINICAL VIGNETTE 19

Bob Dolinski, a borderline young man in twice weekly
psychotherapy, exploded with rage when I refused to
comply with his demand for painkillers. In a menac-
ing tone, he threatened to take my eyeballs out and
crush them under his feet. Alarmed by his emotional
flooding and rapidly disintegrating reality-testing, I
firmly told him to stay put in his chair. I added that if
her as much as laid a finger on me I would terminate

the treatment and never see him again. I told him that
he needed someone who could listen to him peacefully, not someone who was afraid of him and that I
would be afraid of him if he acted even once on his
impulse to hurt me. Noticing that he was settling
down, I added that the idea that he could take my
eyeballs out was both unrealistic and intriguing. He
could not do it; I would not let him. And, why did he
think of eyeballs in the first place? Could it have
something to do with the memory of his mother looking contemptuously at him? Interventions along these
lines calmed him down and soon the session was progressing in a more mutually related manner.

In contrast to the three clinical vignettes offered so far, disruptions of therapeutic frame, at times, happen outside of clinical
hours.

CLINICAL VIGNETTE 20

Ruby Kaplan, a thin-skinned fearful, and immensely
needy, borderline young woman was in a five-times-a-
week analysis. From time to time she felt a bit more
confident of her acceptability to me. Usually this was
a result of a piece of superego analysis, whereby the
defensive nature of her inhibitions became more ob-
servable to her and she learned of the childhood roots
and current uses of terrifying inner injunctions. Mostly, she was afraid of overburdening me and immensely thankful for my attention. At other times, she expressed a need to see me more often, have longer sessions, meet me on demand, and so on. Five times a
week for fifty minutes certainly did not seem enough.
I encouraged her to tell me more about this. She revealed that as a child she felt horribly rejected by her
mother, who sternly discouraged any physical contact
between them. She sobbed. We went on in this staccato fashion.

Then, one day Ruby revealed that she had found
out where I lived and had driven by to take a look at

my house. I experienced mixed feelings upon hearing this. Mostly, I felt fascination at this manner of the transference deepening. The link between this behavior and her childhood wishes to touch her mother was clear to me. When I brought this to her attention, she noticed the connection too. However, the material did not deepen. Inquiries what fantasies she had about my house, what or who she really wanted to see, what the house stood for, how the looking at my house might have been a way of avoiding wishes to see me more fully (she was on the couch) yielded meager results.

Gradually, the pattern of visiting my house became a regular one. Three, four times a week, including weekends, she drove by the street on which I live, slowing down as she passed my house, looking at it intently. Once in a while, from inside my house, I could see her driving by in her car. I felt intruded upon and annoyed. Listening to the reports of these visits during her sessions, I was reminded of her wanting to see me more than five times a week, for longer sessions, and on demand. I wondered if behind such coercive control lurked the fear of having 'killed' me during the intervals? Or, was it a developmental need? In other words, was the patient's wish to have more contact a defense against repressed hostility or was her going to my house an innovative way of having more sessions, without which she felt utterly disorganized? Two interventions were thus possible. One leaned towards interpreting the defensive and/or provocative actions. The other involved acknowledging the adaptive aspects of her behavior, which sought satisfaction of an ego need that I had failed to meet. I chose the latter intervention and it facilitated the progress of our work.[33] The patient felt understood, came up with new memories, and gradually stopped driving by my house.

This list of pained pauses (Clinical Vignette 17), angry with-drawals (Clinical Vignette 18), threats of violence (Clinical Vignette 19), and stalking-like behavior (Clinical Vignette 20), does not ex-haust the manifestations of clinical disruption. Walking out in the middle of sessions, deliberate lateness, not paying bills, destroying property in the therapist's office, and dropping out of treatment constitute other manifestations. Still more behavioral examples can be given, I am sure. What remains common in all these instances, however, is the breakdown of verbal communication and over-throw of the therapeutic alliance by transference acting out.

THERAPEUTIC INTERVENTIONS

While the technical stance vis-à-vis disruptions has found some mention above, I now wish to spell out such matters more explicit-ly. My aim is to highlight five aspects of psychotherapeutic tech-nique that deal directly with episodes of disruption. These points are to be utilized alongside the ordinary therapeutic tasks of listen-ing with empathy and non-judgmental attitude, offering support and clarification, interpreting transferences, and formulating ge-netic reconstructions.

Holding And Containing

The term 'holding environment' was coined by Winnicott in con-nection with the ordinary function of a mother holding her infant. Holding in this context meant 'not only the actual physical holding of the infant, but also the total environmental provision prior to the concept of living with' (p. 43). Winnicott (1960) noted that the hold-ing environment's main function is 'the reduction of impingements to which the infant must react with resultant annihilation of per-sonal being' (p.47). He came to believe that the psychotherapeutic situation should be like such a holding environment and should provide safety, security, an unhurried attitude, and containment of affects and offer an opportunity for one's growth potential to be re-activated. Such metaphorical holding becomes even more impor-tant when the physical continuity of a session is threatened.

A common situation is when a patient abruptly and angrily walks out of a session, slamming the office door behind him. Faced with such a situation, the therapist should neither stay put in his chair nor run after the patient.[34] The former allows the patient's 'attack on the setting' (Limentani, 1989) to rupture the therapeutic connection, and exposes the patient to the humiliation of having to knock on the door should he return. The latter is an impingement on the patient's autonomy, permissible only if there is a serious suicidal risk and not otherwise. Better than either of these options is walking up to the door, opening it, making sure that it stays open, and returning to one's chair. This way the office has been 'extended' to include the hallway or wherever the patient has gone.

Assuring Safety And Setting Limits

The therapist dealing with a truly intense disruption must also take measures to protect the physical safety of the two people involved in the transaction. Suicidal and homicidal crises (and their less malignant versions) must be handled with patience coupled with firm limit-setting. A combination of empathy, resilience, and reality-testing should form the mainstay of the therapist's approach. Use of psychotropic medications might become necessary under such circumstances. However, this requires keeping the following judicious guidelines (Gorton & Akhtar, 1990) in mind.

First, drug treatment should not be presented to patients as a panacea—it is better to profess a cautious uncertainty about possible benefit, even if this attitude mitigates placebo effect. Second, careful consideration should be given to risks versus benefit before instituting medication for patients with ongoing substance abuse, suicidal ideation, or inability to comply with required diet, blood levels, dosing schedule, or follow-up visits. Third, a consistent focus on unrealistic expectations is crucial to maximize both compliance and evaluation of efficacy. Fourth, concurrent treatments should remain firmly in place because drug therapy alone is rarely globally effective. Fifth, drugs should be introduced into treatment as a single variable: they should be used for preplanned periods with a clear beginning, and end-point related to agreed-on target symptoms. Sixth, serial substitution of alternative drugs is preferable to concurrent use of alternative drugs. Seventh, drugs and dosages that may cause tardive dyskinesia, paradoxical dyscontrol, or lowering of seizure threshold should, if possible, be reserved as final treatment options. Eighth, informed consent for drug trials should be obtained continually over the course of treatment. Ninth, worsening symptoms should alert the clinician to the possible presence of some other disorder, a negative therapeutic reaction, a drug interaction with illicit agents, a paradoxical aggravation of target symptoms, or the presence of an undiagnosed medical illness. (p. 47)

Other adjunct measures (e.g. family meetings, hospitalization) should also be considered if the patient's regression is severe and if the disruptive behaviors are approaching dangerous limits.

Naming And Taming

Disruptions accompanied by emotional flooding, danger of in-session violence, and diabolical transformations of the patient's identity should be met with 're-humanizing' attempts on the therapist's part. The therapist should appear calm, not make abrupt movements, and gently but clearly name the affect that the patient is experiencing (Katan, 1961). For instance, the therapist might say 'you are really enraged', or 'you seem to be in unbelievable pain'. Such comments might appear simplistic but the fact is that they give the patient an intellectual handle at a time when his or her ego is getting overwhelmed by affect. If this does not seem sufficient to calm the patient down, the therapist might gently take the patient's first name while talking to him or her (Volkan, 1976).[35] 'Reminding' the patient of who he is in reality can draw a cognitive wedge between the diabolically transformed self and the sector of sanity that still exists under such circumstances.

Oscillating In Accordance With The Patient's Level Of Transferences

Most patients with severe personality disorders fluctuate between integrated and unintegrated levels of ego functioning. At the former, they appear torn and conflicted. At the latter, they seem confident and demanding. This is important to keep in mind since the therapist's approach has to shift according to such alterations in the patient. When the patient's transferences reflect the conflict-based sector of his personality, the technical approach should be one of skeptical listening, search for concealed meanings, and interpretive interventions. But when the patient's transferences reflect deficit-based sectors of his personality, the technical approach should be characterized by credulous listening, validation of the patient's psychic reality, and affirmation interventions (Killingmo, 1989). At such moments 'issues of subtle meaning, affect, and wish, are of secondary importance to the issues of internal intactness' (Greenspan, 1977, p.387). In other words, holding, facilitating, containing and surviving matter more at such moments than deciphering and interpreting on the analyst's part.

Designating these two poles of technique 'maternal' and 'paternal' and tracing them back to Winnicott's and Freud's therapeutic styles respectively, Wright (1991) declared that they 'provide a point and counterpoint in analysis between two styles and two visions and neither wins the day completely' (p. 200). The therapist has to learn to oscillate between affirmative and interpretive aspects of technique and such oscillations should be in harmony with patient's movements of regression and progression (Killingmo, 1989).

Acknowledging One's Own Role In Precipitating A Disruption

When an honest bit of soul searching on the therapist's part reveals that he might have contributed to occurrence of a disruption, this must be explicitly acknowledged and conveyed to the patient. By so doing, the therapist (a) provides the patient with an experience of having effectively communicated his distress to the analyst; this results in a self-enhancing experience of efficacy, and (b) restores the patient's experience of a positive bond with the analyst. A comment indicating one's understanding of the patient's suffering often leads to further progress in psychotherapy.

> The acknowledgment by the analyst of his having been experienced by the analysand in such a way as to trigger the disruption usually leads to a collaborative inquiry by both into the dynamic and genetic causes of the disruption. For the analysand this becomes an experience of being understood, an experience of efficacy in having an influence on the analyst,

and, finally, an experience of being vitalized by the affective attunement with the analyst. (Wolf, 1994, pp.
94-95)

While an acknowledgment of one's lapse in empathy is often
sufficient, in situations where the therapist's 'mistake' is gross, an
apology might be indicated. This is a controversial matter to be
sure. Goldberg (1987), in discussing the place of apology in psychoanalysis, delineates two possible stances. One stance, exempli-
fied in the clinical material previously mentioned, emanates from
the analytic perspective which suggests that via empathic immer-
sion, the analyst may attain an ability to see the patient's world as
he or she does *and* the major burden of achieving and sustaining
such intersubjective agreement rests upon the analyst. In this view
the failure of intersubjectivity would largely be the analyst's responsibility and thus necessitate an apology from the analyst. The
second stance, mentioned by Goldberg, argues the untenability of
either extreme position, concluding that while the wish to apologize may be countertransference based, it does have a place at certain times in certain treatments. Of course, the patient's experience
of the analyst's apology needs then to be explored and handled in
a relatively traditional way.

A DEVELOPMENTAL POSTSCRIPT

The therapist dealing with individuals prone to disruptions must
remember that, developmentally speaking, disruption is not an exception but a rule. Traced through the life span, one can observe
that (a) the onset of the differentiation phase of separation-individuation disrupts the calm of symbiosis, and the rapprochement
phase destabilizes the euphoric self-reliance of the practicing phase
proper (Mahler et al., 1975); (b) the discovery of anatomical differences between sexes (Freud, 1925) puts an uncomfortable end to
the ignorant bliss of the preceding era; (c) the beginning of adolescence (Blos, 1967; Erikson, 1950) abruptly terminates the playful
equanimity of latency; and (d) the arrival of middle age, with its
own characteristic psychosocial challenges (Kernberg, 1980),
shakes up the hitherto coherent adulthood. What all this tells us is
that psychic development continues throughout life (Pine, 1997)

and occurs in a dialectics of 'noisy' and 'non-noisy' phases (Leaff, 1991). The former introduce new developmental tasks, and the latter synthesize and consolidate these gains. The same applies to psychotherapy.

Another developmental matter is pertinent in this context. This involves the fact that the technical polarities of listening with credulousness (and responding with affirmative interventions) versus listening with skepticism (and responding with interpretive interventions) are akin to the maternal and paternal styles of relating to young children. Herzog's (1984) elucidation of the 'homeostatic' and 'disruptive' attunements of parents to their growing child is especially illuminating here. Through video-monitored child-observational studies, Herzog has demonstrated that mothers usually join in with a toddler in his or her ongoing play (e.g. building a tower with wooden blocks), thus giving the child a 'continuity of being' (Winnicott, 1965, p.54), validity and harmony with the environment ('homeostatic attunement'). Fathers, on the contrary, characteristically disrupt the playing toddler's equilibrium by cajoling him or her into joining them in a new activity ('disruptive attunement'). Homeostatic attunement has affirming qualities necessary for the sustenance and consolidation of self-experience. Disruptive attunement has enhancing qualities necessary for the broadening and deepening of self-experience. The influence of the two types of attunements is additive and contributes to a healthy self-experience. Herzog further observed that fathers distract the child from the game he or she is playing only when mother is with the child. In her absence, and especially with younger children, fathers too start playing the child's own game (i.e. resort to homeostatic attunement). This suggests that homeostatic attunement is an experiential prerequisite for disruptive attunement.[36]

Extrapolating these developmental observations to the clinical situation suggests the following. The analyst's credulous listening and 'affirmative' (Killingmo, 1989) interventions are akin to the maternal 'homeostatic attunement' insofar as they too aim to validate, strengthen, and stabilize the self-experience. The analyst's skepticism regarding the patient's conscious material and his unmasking interpretive interventions seem akin to the paternal 'disruptive attunement' insofar as these too cause cognitive expansion by introducing new material into the patient's awareness. Herzog's conclusion that homeostatic attunement is a prerequisite for the disruptive attunement also finds a parallel in the clinical situation wherein the analyst's holding and affirmative functions must be securely in place in order for his interpretive efforts to be fruitful. Couched in this developmental metaphor, the analyst's exercise of maternal functions seems to be a prerequisite for his or her exercise of paternal functions. Applied specifically to episodes of disruption, one can say that the patient's inner sense of the therapeutic relationship must be stabilized before he can utilize interpretations which, by definition, bring something new to the patient's attention and slightly destabilize him. The patient must be helped to regain a 'safety feeling' (Sandler, 1960) before the risk of encountering the repudiated aspects of his self-experience.

Finally, it should also be remembered that the capacity to cause a disruption might itself be a developmental advance on the part of the patient. In other words, a meek and previously unentitled individual might begin experiencing enhanced self esteem as a result of treatment and this, in turn, might lead to his making more overt attacks on the therapeutic boundaries. Winnicott's (1956) notion that outrageousness is often a sign of unconscious hope (of finding an accepting and tolerant environment) is pertinent in this context.

CLINICAL VIGNETTE 21

Nina Ghosh, a forty year-old woman with an 'as if' personality (Deutsch, 1942), was in twice-weekly psychotherapy with me. She had grown up living with rigid rules and constant efforts at appeasing others. As the treatment progressed, it became clear that her profoundly disinterested parents (and, her caretakers subsequent to their death when the patient was four years old) had not imparted to her any sense of confidence and healthy entitlement. Gradually, in her work with me, the patient began to experience enhanced self-esteem and to express criticism of me when it came to her mind. She liked this newly found freedom very much and once, while angry with me, deliberately did not show up for our session. In light of her psychopathology, I saw this disruptive behavior as not only an ego advance on the patient's part but also as

an evidence that the treatment was indeed progressing well.

CONCLUDING REMARKS

In this chapter, I have defined the concept of 'disruption', outlined
its dynamics, described its manifestations, and elucidated psychotherapeutic techniques to deal with it. In doing so, I have cast
my net wide and included both psychiatric and psychoanalytic
perspectives. Moreover, in describing the dynamics of clinical disruptions, I have tried to account for variables from within the patient as well as from within the therapist. Throughout all of this, I
have kept an eye on in-depth subjectivity as well as developmental
prototypes. My hope is that what I have offered here will help the
therapists of disruption-prone patients bear and understand clinical crises in a more meaningful way. It might also prepare them to
manage those situations better where the patient seems intent
upon self-destruction. The next chapter addresses this matter in
greater depth.

5. SUICIDAL CRISES

*That is what chills your spine when you read an account of a suicide: not
the frail corpse hanging from the window bars but what happened
inside that heart immediately before.*

Simone de Beauvoir (1908-1986)

The possibility of someone committing suicide is a major psychiatric emergency. All mental health clinicians encounter this
emergency at some point or other in their practice. They feel challenged, threatened, scared, and—at times—shaken to their core by
such an experience. Seeing someone about to take his or her own
life stirs up all sorts of clinical, moral, legal and philosophical
dilemmas. To put it plainly: dealing with persons intent upon
killing themselves is not easy.

It is therefore important that mental health clinicians be wellversed in matters involving suicide. Acquiring familiarity with epidemiological, phenomenological, psychodynamic, psychotherapeutic, legal, and moral issues will not make them omnipotent rescuers. However, it can increase the chances of their understanding
the suicidal individual better and therefore helping him in a more
efficient way. It is with this goal in mind that I offer the following
considerations. Not aiming for a comprehensive review of literature on suicide, I will nonetheless draw from significant earlier
writings to highlight pertinent dynamic themes as well as therapeutic and preventive strategies in this realm.

119

WHAT DOES THE EPIDEMIOLOGY OF SUICIDE TEACH US?

As psychotherapists, we focus upon one particular person's dynamics at a time. We strive to learn about the hereditary legacies, childhood environment, internal dynamics, ego assets and vulnerabilities, superego pressures, and contemporary burdens that are specific to this particular individual; this helps us evolve strategies to help him or her. Specificity is the motto of our workshop. Matters of epidemiology and statistics are of little interest to us. Yet, the fact remains that 'macroscopic' data of this sort can also equip us to become better diagnosticians and therapists. It therefore cannot be ignored. In the realm of suicide, for instance, the following epidemiologically derived information merits our serious consideration.

- Approximately 30,000 people kill themselves each year in the United States (Roy, 2000). This does not include those who arrange to get themselves killed (e.g. provoke homicide or die in unconsciously engineered accidents.)

- About thirty to fifty percent of those who commit suicide are in some form of psychiatric treatment, hence amenable to intervention (Bush & Fawcett, 2004).

- Suicide rates are not universally the same. Incidence of suicide is higher in Austria, Germany, Japan, and Switzerland. It is lower in Holland, Italy, and Norway, and strikingly low in Ireland, Brazil, and Spain (Weiss, 1974).

- Suicide attempts are more prevalent in women, completed suicides in men. This is most likely because men have greater access to firearms and, in general, use more violent means while attempting suicide (Roy, 2000).

- Suicide rates and homicide rates are often inversely related by cities and other regions, and in periods of economic prosperity and depression (Weiss, 1974).

- Generally speaking, the age group most vulnerable to suicide is between 55 to 65 years (Weiss, 1974; Roy, 2000). However, the alarming increase in suicide rates noted recently among teenage, ghetto-based, poor African-American males (Poussaint & Alexander, 2000) might alter this statistic.

- The peak time for suicide is on Sundays or around major holidays (McCulloch & Philip, 1972).

- Suicide is more common among single, divorced, widowed, childless, and physically ill individuals (Dublin, 1963; Fareberow & Shneidman, 1961; Roy, 2000).

- Physicians and especially psychiatrists have a higher incidence of suicide than the general population (Hawton et al., 2001; Stack, 2004).

A careful look at this data reveals considerable information of psychodynamic significance. It shows that modal child-rearing practices that are harshly anti-instinctual and shame-inducing (see the countries with high suicide rates), greater aggression (see the gender difference in suicide rates), a sense of hopelessness and feeling trapped (e.g. poor African-American men), social isolation (e.g. divorced and widowed individuals), and being chronically burdened with caretaking responsibilities (e.g. physicians) put one at a greater risk of considering and/or committing suicide. However, such inferences drawn from the broad strokes of epidemiology only prepare us to look for patterns of vulnerability in the clinical situation. Deeper knowledge of what contemplating suicide is about comes to us only from listening to our patients.

PSYCHODYNAMIC UNDERPINNINGS

The psychodynamics of suicidal threats and acts, like all other mental phenomena, is multiply-determined (Waelder, 1936). A single cause is hardly ever sufficient to result in suicide. In almost all instances, a number of variables are simultaneously active in causing suicidal behavior. For instance, issues of sadomasochism (an id variable), compromised reality-testing and weakened impulse control (an ego variable), guilt-driven need for self-punishment (a superego variable), feelings of shame and humiliation (an ego-ideal variable), and hopelessness born out of socioeconomic hardship (an external reality based variable) can work synergistically and contribute to the final common pathway of suicide. The degree to which one or the other factor is predominant in any given case varies greatly and so do the permutations and combinations of the various factors listed above.

Also worth keeping in mind is that the individual contemplating suicide might not be thinking of actually dying.[37] Motives other than a wish to die (e.g. the wish to kill someone, who unfortunately has come to reside within oneself) can also lead to suicidal actions. Even in the instances where there is a clear wish to die, the wish to survive persists side-by-side. 'Most people who commit suicidal acts do not want either to die or to live; they want to do both at the same time, usually the one more, or much more, than the other' (Stengel, 1964, p. 87). Moreover, people's concept of death might itself lack a sense of finality. Indeed, approximately 85 percent of people in this country believe in some form of continuing life (e.g. going to heaven or hell, persistence of the soul in one form or another, reincarnation) after death (Newsweek-Beliefnet Survey, cited in Adler, 2005). Even outside of such spiritual beliefs, many people 'seem to have the idea that death is a form of sleep, some sort of refreshing repose from which they will awaken with all their problems having been resolved' (Bellak & Faithorn, 1981 p.71). Death does not mean the end of life for them. Such self-deceptions might facilitate what, at its core, must be an enormously difficult and heart-wrenching task, namely to give up on one's own life. Pondering this difficulty, Freud (1910) stated the following:

> We are anxious above all to know how it becomes possible for the extraordinary powerful life instinct to be overcome: whether this can only come about with the help of a disappointed libido or whether the ego can renounce its self-preservation for its own egoistic motives. (p. 232)

Of the two motives for suicide mentioned by Freud, the former received more attention in the subsequent literature. His notion of 'disappointed libido' gave rise to the widely prevalent thinking that loss of instinctual gratification (or, more accurately the refusal to accept such loss) can lead to suicide. Situations of unrequited love, break-up of romantic relationships, as well as the death of a loved one fall into this category of precipitating factors. All of them lead to severe id frustrations. This much is clear in Freud's exposition. What remained unstated there, yet seems possible, is that the 'disappointed libido' might also be a reflection of a weak ego. In other words, a socially inept and hapless individual might be unable to extract adequate emotional nourishment from this world, feel deeply wounded, and give up on life. Of course, it can be argued the 'weak ego' underlying such social ineffectiveness is itself an end-product of neglect, deprivation, and harshness experienced during childhood. A 'disappointed libido' creates a weak ego and a weak ego, in turn, leads to further libidinal frustrations. The following observation by Ferenczi (1929) elegantly captures this situation:

> Children who received in a harsh and unloving way die easily and willingly. Either they use one of the many proffered organic possibilities for a quick exit, or if they escape this fate, they retain a streak of pessimism and aversion to life. (p. 105)

The second factor mentioned by Freud, namely, renunciation of self preservation for 'egoistic motives', received far less attention by subsequent analysts though it is my sense that Winnicott (1960) did pick up this theme in his reflections on suicide. However, before going in that direction, let me mention Freud's later elaboration of the dynamics of suicidal tendencies. In his seminal paper 'Mourning and Melancholia' (1917), Freud stated that:

> the ego can kill itself only, if owing to the return of object cathexis, it can treat itself as an object—if it is able to direct against itself the hostility which relates to an object and which represents the ego's original reaction to objects in the external world. (p. 252)

This view of suicide as a 'retroflexed murder' gradually replaced the 'disappointed libido' hypothesis and became the centerpiece of psychoanalytic thought on suicide. The implicit category of 'sadistic' suicide grew and took over almost all the terrain of severe self-destructive actions. The formula that in killing oneself, one was actually attacking a hostile internal object was given support by the views of many subsequent psychoanalysts (Abraham, 1924; Bernfeld, 1929; Klein 1935; Kernberg 1975, 1984). An unfortunate result of this emphasis was that the comparatively passive version of this dynamic received short shrift. In other words, emphasis upon the view that suicide was a murder *of* a bad internal object eclipsed the fact that suicide was also a murder of the self *by* a bad internal object. This despite the fact that such surrender to a powerful object had been noted in a striking sentence by Freud in the same 1917 paper. He stated that: 'in the two opposed situations of being most intensely in love and of suicide, the ego is overwhelmed by the object, though in totally different ways' (p. 252). In love, the ego gives itself over to an idealized, 'good' object and in suicide to an exalted, 'bad' object. This laid the groundwork for Freud's (1920, 1923) still later view of suicide as a culmination of a guilty need for self-punishment. This was 'masochistic' suicide par excellence.

While agreeing that attacks against and by bad internal objects play an important role in causing suicide, Klein (1935) proposed an additional possibility. She stated that the suicidal individual

> hates not only his 'bad' objects, but his id as well and that vehemently. In committing suicide, his purpose may be to make a clean breach in his relation to the outside world because his desires to rid some real object—or the 'good' object which that whole world represents and which the ego is identified with—of himself, or of that part of his ego which is identified with his bad objects and his id. (p. 276)

This is a 'morally-clean', altruistic suicide, so to speak. It comprises of self-destruction in order to avoid burdening others by one's needs and demands. Many suicides in the context of incurable and terminal illness fall in this category. However, the border between a guilt-ridden conclusion that one is a burden upon others and a genuine appraisal of one's extraordinary needs being hard for others to meet is often a blurred one, to say the least.

In contrast to such potentially altruistic acts of self-destruction are what, for the lack of a better term, might be called 'egoistic' or 'narcissistic' suicides. Freud's question whether the ego can renounce its self-preservation for 'its own egotistic motives' (1910, p. 232) pertains to this type of situation. Paraphrasing him, one might ask whether suicide can actually result from poignant scenarios of genuine self-concern? Here enters Winnicott, who in a provocative passage, touches upon this very matter:

> The False Self has as its main concern a search for conditions which will make it possible for the True Self to come into its own. If conditions cannot be found then there must be reorganized a new defence against exploitation of the True Self, and if there be doubt then the clinical result is suicide. Suicide in this context is the destruction of the total self in avoidance of annihilation of the True Self. When suicide is the only defence left against betrayal of the True Self, then it becomes the lot of the False Self to organize the suicide. This, of course, involves its own destruction, but at the same time eliminates the need for its continued existence, since its function is the protection of the True Self from insult. (1960, p. 143)

The question whether this is 'narcissistic' indulgence or 'self-directed altruism' is clinically and morally challenging. Its answer depends upon the context in which a dynamic of 'preserving the true self' is applied and the philosophical orientation of the one who is making the assessment of the situation. Where do suicidal acts of political martyrdom fit in, for instance? Do they belong among 'altruistic' or among 'egoistic' suicides? What, if any, is the proportion of sadism and masochism in such instances? And, above all, who has the moral authority to decide such matters?

These perplexing issues notwithstanding, Menninger's (1938) views on suicide also need mention in this psychodynamic discourse. According to him, suicidal acts emanate from three sets of motives: (i) the wish not to exist, (ii) the wish to kill, and (iii) the wish to die. They have to do with lives burdened by ego defects, suppressed rage, and profound guilt, respectively. In today's noso-logically-oriented terminology, we would perhaps call them the schizoid, borderline, and depressive motivations, respectively, knowing full well that in actual clinical practice, admixtures of such factors are more common than their pure isolated forms. Nonetheless knowing them could help the therapist evolve match-ing therapeutic strategies. He might direct his attention, for in-stance, towards providing auxiliary support for patients with ego defects. He might help contain the fuming affects and explore the reasons for their existence in individuals suffused with impotent rage. He might make unmasking and interpreting interventions in the case of those replete with fantasies leading to guilty self recrim-inations.

All in all, the psychodynamics underlying a suicidal act turns out to be a complex and multifactorial matter. If one gets seduced by a single factor etiological model, then all sorts of categories (e.g. 'sadistic', 'masochistic', 'altruistic', 'egoistic') of suicide present themselves as easy ways out of the psychodynamic conundrum. If one avoids such simplifications, then all suicidal acts appear overdetermined and the treatment strategies for such individuals far from simple.

ASSESSMENT OF SUICIDE RISK

Assessment of suicide risk is not an easy matter. Even the 'stan-dard' suicide risk factors (e.g. depression, hopelessness, social iso-lation, previous suicide attempts) have 'high sensitivity in identify-ing suicidal patients but low specificity in determining which pa-tients will commit suicide' (Simon, 2004, p. 26). Most depressed pa-tients, for instance, do not kill themselves and many people who do are not clinically depressed. The situation is further complicated by the lack of a standardized risk prediction scale to identify which patients will actually commit suicide (Busch et al., 1993) and even if such a scale existed it is unlikely that someone intent upon grievous self-harm will sit down and fill out a psychosocial ques-tionnaire.

The consequence of all this is that perfect suicide risk assessment is not possible. Yet an evaluation of suicidality must be done in order to decide upon further steps in treatment of patients in acute turmoil. Such evaluation should be guided by the consensus recommendations of major professional organizations (e.g. American Psychiatric Association, 2003). It should take into consideration the data that forms the epidemiological background as well as the specific patient under consideration. Moreover, it should include risk factors as well as protective variables (Mago et al., 2004; Simon, 2004). The juxtaposition of these two (e.g. hopelessness as a risk factor versus religious conviction against killing oneself) forms the crucible of clinical thinking in such circumstances. Suicide risk assessment is a process, not an event.

One thing is certain. Simply asking the patient about suicidal ideation, intent, and presence or absence of a plan of action is not sufficient. Majority of individuals who commit suicide do not acknowledge their intent during their final appointment (Isometsa et al., 1995) and many have no specific plan before impulsively committing suicide (Hall et al., 1999). Moreover, those who are intent upon killing themselves seem 'possessed' by an 'internal saboteur' (Fairbain, 1952) and tend to view mental health professionals as the enemy.

In light of such complexities, the clinician would benefit by keeping the following points in mind:

- Suicidal ideation is a key risk factor. A suicidal plan is even more significant. In the National Comorbidity Survey, the probability of transition from ideation to attempt was 26 percent and from plan to attempt 72 percent (Kessler et al., 1999).

- The cause of suicide is multifactorial and so should be the assessment of its risk. In other words, a broader, biopsychosocial assessment (e.g. affective state, degree of impulsivity, presence or absence of substance abuse and excessive drinking, physical health status, recent changes in life situation and protective factors such as good alliance with a therapist or genuine concern about one's family) is more useful than identifying 'standard' suicidal markers alone: suicidal ideation, previous suicide attempts, and hopelessness.

- These three predictors of suicide suggest a *chronic* risk. They are *not* good predictors of acute risk. Suicide can occur in the absence of these predictors.

- Severe anxiety, agitated depression, recent onset of or increase in drinking, panic attacks, and global insomnia are better indicators for *acute* risk (Fawcett, 2001).

- Denial of suicidal intent in the presence of excessive drinking, panic attacks, and global insomnia is *not* reliable (Fawcett, 2001).

- Patients with major affective disorders, chronic alcoholism, schizophrenia, and borderline personality disorder are at a greater risk for suicide (Simon, 2004).

- Finally, triggers for mobilizing suicidal despair, methods of communicating suicidal intent, and protective factors against actual suicide are highly individualized. As a result, a through knowledge of the individual's history, psychodynamics, and overall idiom of life is essential for meaningful assessment of suicide risk.

THERAPEUTIC INTERVENTIONS

Suicidality, especially in its chronic form, often forms the focus of psychotherapeutic dialogue with borderline and depressed patients. It can also occupy considerable conversational space in the treatment of other individuals. Narcissistic patients, for instance, gradually begin to realize the futility of their grandiose pursuits and recognize the hurts they have caused to their friends, lovers, and relatives (Kernberg, 1975); this stirs up powerful feelings of remorse and can mobilize suicidal tendencies. Thoughts of self-destruction can also arise, at times with alarming vehemence, in those who find themselves characterologically unable to love, trapped in profoundly ungratifying marriages, incapable of reversing major life decisions that they have come to regret, and so on. While therapeutic strategies have to be invariably individualized, keeping the following measures in mind can be helpful to the psychotherapist.

Holding And Containing The Patient's Turmoil

The therapist listening to a patient talk about suicide must maintain an attitude of equanimity, non-judgmental seriousness, and patience. He has to remember that, in the realm of suicide, like in any other area of human experience, 'fantasy is not tantamount to the act and that a major therapeutic task is to assist in the construction of a boundary between feeling and fantasy on the one hand and impulsive action on the other' (Lewin & Schulz, 1992, p. 238).

The capacity of the therapist to 'peacefully' listen to patients verbalize suicidal ideation paradoxically strengthens the boundary between thought and action. It is important to remember that the patient needs to extrude (and thus 'share') the forces that threaten his existence from within. 'Suicidality is much more than the search for the doorway to death' (Lewin & Schulz, 1992, p.240). The therapist's 'holding' (Winnicott, 1960) and 'containing' (Bion, 1967) functions give the patient implicit permission to express powerful affects in the clinical situation. This improves the patient's capacity to assess and understand his inner and outer realities. With the dreaded agenda out in the open, there is a diminution of shame and sense of aloneness. Dynamic exploration then becomes possible. Crucial is the therapist's ability to:

> empathize with the patient's suicide temptations, with his longing for peace, with his excitement of self-directed aggression, with his pleasure in taking revenge against significant others, with his wish to escape from guilt, and with the exhilarating sense of power involved in suicidal urges. Only that kind of empathy on the part of the therapist may permit the patient to explore these issues openly in treatment. (Kernberg, 1984, p. 263)

Setting Limits While Retaining An Interpretative Approach

When matters begin to get out of hand, however, the therapist should resort to limit-setting. This is not opposed to 'holding'; in fact, firmness of therapeutic stance might be seen as an assertive form of 'holding'. The developmental prototype of the two is the support-expectation paradigm inherent in all good parenting. The parent offers help to the child but also expects appropriate behavior from him or her.

The patient's suicidal ideas should be listened to peacefully within the context of a therapeutic alliance but, when the patient loses such rapport, becomes too depressed to communicate, or begins to make practical arrangements for committing suicide, he or she must be actively protected. The therapist must take 'responsible action, with or without the patient's approval' (Kernberg et al., 1989, p. 155).

CLINICAL VIGNETTE 22

Sarah Green, a forty-five year-old librarian made an appointment to see me upon her sister's insistence. She appeared overwhelmed with pain at the break up of a romantic relationship. Having lived alone most of her life, she found this belated attachment profoundly significant. The man she was involved with was married. He abruptly left her saying that he could no longer continue cheating on his wife. She was destroyed. Heartbroken, she came to see me.

We began the first hour of consultation in a customary history-taking way. However, within twenty minutes of the session, she announced that she had decided to blow her head off with a gun which she had bought earlier that day. Alarmed by the earnestness of her tone, I suggested that we take immediate steps to get the gun removed from her apartment, obtain some collateral information regarding the extent of her depression, and consider beginning our work on an inpatient basis. The patient reacted sharply to my suggestion and, refusing to let me contact her sister who could remove the gun, got up to leave the office. At this point, I said to her: 'Look, everybody gets about ten candles worth of life and inside you eight have already gone out. The wind is blowing hard and to protect the remaining two candles, you came here and put them in my heart. Now, since you have enlisted me for this purpose, it is my duty to keep these two candles protected from the wind. When the storm settles, I will return them to you so that you can light the other eight candles back with their help.' The patient broke down in tears and after some thinking gave me the permission to contact her sister who subsequently removed the gun from the patient's apartment and encouraged the patient to stay at her house for the next few days.

As this example shows, the behavioral limit-setting is to be combined, as much as possible, with some degree of interpretation of the potential meanings of the patient's impulses and actions. Otherwise, the patient can receive an impression that all the therapist is interested in is his behavior and not the subjective distress that underlies it. Worse, the patient comes to believe that threatening suicide has inordinate power over the therapist and can be used for sadistic purposes in the transference (Kernberg et al., 1989). Continuing to interpret while setting limits demonstrates to the patient that the therapist's analyzing function has not been compromised under the influence of the former's regression.

Utilizing Adjunct Measures

Psychotherapists dealing with suicidal patients should realize that there are situations when one-to-one psychotherapy is simply not enough to contain the psychosocial distress involved. They should be comfortable deploying adjunct measures, including the enlistment of a family member's help, use of psychotropic medications, and hospitalization of the patient.

Involvement Of Family Members

When a patient seems unable to contain his suicidal impulses enough to make them a topic of continued psychotherapeutic exploration (e.g. *Who* do you really want to kill? *What* are you so hopeless about? How do you think this talk is affecting *me*? and so on), the therapist should ask the patient's permission to involve his family members in managing the crisis. If the patient refuses, the therapist should inform him that he will seek appropriate legal counsel (e.g. from one's professional organization's legal division, or one's hospital's risk-management department) and might have to break confidentiality to protect the patient's life.

When a family meeting can be arranged, the therapist must inform those gathered of the following: (a) that the patient suffers from a psychological condition with a definite risk of self-induced mortality,[38] and (b) that while the therapist would work earnestly and in the best of his or her capacity to help the patient overcome these emotional problems, he cannot guarantee that the treatment would be successful or that the danger of suicide would be averted forever.

> This realistic circumscription of the treatment may be the most effective way to protect the therapeutic relationship from the destructive involvements of the family members and from the patient's efforts to control the therapy by inducing in the therapist a countertransference characterized by guilt feelings and paranoid fears regarding third parties. (Kernberg, et al., 1989, p. 157)

It is only with such understanding in place that the treatment of chronically suicidal individuals should be continued. In its absence, legally appropriate measures should be resorted to, to terminate the treatment and refer the patient elsewhere. Continuing treatment under unrealistic circumstances worsens countertransference difficulties and these, in turn, make treatment even more problematic.

Use Of Medications

While depressed patients with suicidal tendencies would most likely already be on antidepressant medications and bipolar affective disorder patients on mood stabilizers (e.g. lithium, divalproex sodium), there is growing evidence these medications exert little 'anti-suicidal' effect for about six months (Bush & Fawcett, 2004). The acute risk of suicide is better treated with long-acting benzodiazepines or atypical antipsychotic agents (Jacobs & Brewer, 2004). The caveats outlined by Gorton and Akhtar (1988) and cited in detail in the previous chapter should also be kept in mind.

Hospitalization

For acutely suicidal patients with limited social supports, brief hospitalization can prove to be life-saving. Provision of a safe and tender 'holding environment' (Winnicott, 1960) can tame the affective outburst, mobilize social supports, improve the patient's capacity to think clearly, and allow time for dynamic exploration of the inner turmoil. It is when the patient—characteristically showing up in the emergency room just as the weekend is about to begin (owing to increased separation anxiety, heightened fear of aloneness and boredom, and jealousy of the therapist's real or imagined weekend companions)—is dubiously suicidal that the decision to hospitalize or not hospitalize appears especially confusing.

Kernberg (1984) has provided some useful pointers in this regard. According to him, assessment of the patient's degree of honesty and self-concern is of extreme importance under such circumstances. The former would indicate whether any 'contract' made with him to not hurt himself till the next clinical visit can be deemed reliable or not. The latter would indicate whether the patient, if not hospitalized, is likely to seek the help of others or even come back to the emergency room if he or she gets more desperate. In addition to these two variables, the presence or absence of drinking, substance abuse and possession of firearms should also be investigated. Social isolation and major physical illness also can tilt the prognosis negatively.

A paradox appears at this point. The suicidal patient who is honest, self-concerned, does not drink or abuse drugs, is physically healthy, does not possess a gun, and has reasonable family support will evoke more positive feelings from the evaluating therapist. The suicidal patient who is the opposite in all these ways will stir up negative feelings in the evaluating therapist. And yet it is the latter who is in greater need of hospitalization. The very fact that he is capable of mobilizing intense negative countertransference shows that his inner world is full of a greater amount of self-loathing. To put it in simple words: the therapist's 'dislike' of the patient is a paradoxical indicator of the need for hospitalization.

Countertransference Reactions

Chronically self-destructive patients, especially those who make repeated suicidal attempts, evoke much countertransference upheaval. The suicidal borderline patient makes demands for extra sessions, repeated phone conversations, anxiolytic medications, and physical contact. They frequently project their 'bad' internal objects into the therapist, accusing him of being unloving, withholding, unempathic, sarcastic, or outright cruel (Kernberg, 1984; Kernberg et al., 1989). They get enraged at the therapist's having a separate life; they want to be his 'number one' person and, barring that, feel painfully excluded and hateful.

Emotional burdens on the therapist come from other sources as well. Having to recognize that months and, at times, years of devoted attention and patience can readily be reduced to shreds by the patient, is not easy. Also difficult is bearing repeated angry assaults upon oneself. Real and imagined fears of 'third parties' bringing legal suits against oneself in case the patient does commit suicide are also burdensome. All this takes its toll and the therapist begins to feel anger towards the patient.

Countertransference of this sort might gradually build up to the extent that the therapist begins hating the patient. This consists of both aversion and malice, though one of these might be more conscious than the other. Aversion leads to the wish to withdraw from the patient and abandon him. Malice leads to cruel impulses toward the patient, manifesting as sarcasm, deliberate withholding, and even directly hurtful actions. Viewing himself as a caring individual, the therapist is vulnerable to mobilize unconscious defenses against such countertransference feelings.

Maltsberger and Buie (1974) have outlined five such defensive postures: (i) *Repression.* This might give rise to lack of interest in working with the patient, chronic boredom, day-dreaming during the sessions, frequently and obviously looking at the clock, and worse still, forgetting the patient's appointments. (ii) *Turning against the self.* The analyst using this defense becomes doubtful about his skills, excessively self-critical, and masochistically submissive to the patient. This last-mentioned tendency is more marked in those analysts who are characterologically prone to guilt and self-punishment. (iii) *Distortion and denial of reality for validation of countertransference hatred.* In order to rationalize his hatred, the analyst might distort clinical facts and ignore important information. As a result, he might transfer, prematurely discharge, or altogether abandon the patient. (iv) *Projection.* Here the therapist begins to dread that the patient will commit suicide. 'This kind of preoccupation is usually accompanied by some degree of fear (the consequence of projected malice), and with a degree of aversion, i.e., the patient seems abominable' (Maltsberger & Buie, 1974, p. 629). (v) *Reaction formation.* The analyst using reaction formation might become excessively helpful ('pitiless hospitality' in Salman Rushdie's terms) with omnipotent rescue fantasies and unrealistic interventions in the patient's real life. The defensive nature of such therapeutic zeal is betrayed not only by its anxious rigidity but often by its results as well. The following observations of Searles (1967) capture such developments in a pithy manner:

> The suicidal patient, who finds us so unable to be aware of the murderous feelings he fosters in us through his guilt-and-anxiety-producing threats of suicide, feels increasingly constricted, perhaps indeed to the point of suicide, by the therapist who, in reaction formation against his intensifying, unconscious wishes to kill the patient, hovers increasingly 'protectively' about him, for whom he feels an omnipotence-based physicianly concern. Hence it is, paradoxically, the very physician most anxiously concerned to keep the patient alive who is tending most vigorously, at an unconscious level, to drive him to what has come to seem the only autonomous act left to him—suicide. (p.131)

Clearly one hopes that the problematic countertransference reactions described by Searles (1967) and Maltsberger and Buie (1974) do not occur very often. Much more desirable is that the therapist does not bury his hatred deep into his unconscious but lets it emerge into his conscious awareness. While this does not eliminate the deleterious impact of this hatred on his analytic ego altogether, it does permit him to work his way through this difficult experience. At worst, the therapist continues to oscillate between emotionally giving up on the patient and attempting to re-solve the patient's hatred analytically. Indeed, these oscillations may reflect 'a reasonable compromise formation that permits the therapist to step back and evaluate the effects of his various inter-ventions and gives him some breathing space before he returns to an active interpretive stance' (Kernberg, 1992, p. 31).

RESPONDING TO SUICIDAL THREATS ON THE PHONE

Responding to a phone call in the middle of the night by a patient who is threatening to commit suicide is a challenging task. Most textbooks on psychotherapy and psychoanalysis do not provide guidelines for what might be an appropriate way of dealing with such a situation. Fortunately, Hellinga, van Luwyn and Dalewijk's (2000) collection of interviews with thirteen clinicians dealing with severe personality disorders contains their responses to the follow-ing question: 'In the middle of the night, you are called on the phone by a patient who threatens to commit suicide. What would you do in such a situation?' (p. 18). Personal, anecdotal, and less than 'scientific' though these might be, they are currently our only source of information in this regard. Here are three selected quota-tions:

> *Gerald Adler:* A patient of mine? Then I would know something about him or her and it probably would not come out of the blue. Knowing something about the dynamics of the person, what's going on in his life and where we are in the treatment, I would obviously take it seriously and wonder why I was getting this call at that time of night. If I really thought we were dealing with a life or death situation, I would be will-ing to talk with the person then. Not in the office, but on the phone, even for longer than half an hour if it were necessary. (Cited in Hellinga et al., 2000, p. 18)

> *Glen Gabbard:* It would depend on the nature of the al-liance with the patient, the issue of base-line suicidali-ty, and the frequency with which the patient has called me before. In general, I will say to a suicidal

borderline patient, 'If you feel that you are so out of control that you might act on the suicidal wishes, I want you to call me, even if it is in the middle of the night'. If they abuse that and call me frequently, I will set limits and say to them in the session, 'I cannot work with you if you wake me up frequently at night. I will lie awake worrying about you and the next day I will be too tired to think well. So we have to work out a different way of doing this'. With a person who did it once in a great while, I would be concerned that this person was very seriously suicidal and get them to a hospital. (Cited in Hellinga et al., 2000, p, 149)

Otto Kernberg: It depends on whether it is a patient of mine or some one else's. One who is in treatment with me? Then if he is severely depressed, if the suicide is part of depression, I hospitalize the patient. If it is characterological and he threatens me with it, as he has done ten or more times before, I remind him of the contract: either he controls it or he goes to a hospital. If this patient has swallowed enough to make dying a possibility, I'll do everything to save his life. If this is the first time, I go in and save his life and tell him, 'If you do this once more, the therapy will stop'. If it is the second time, I go, save his life and then refer him to somebody else. I have no problem with that. (Cited in Hellinga et al., 2000, p. 175)

My own response to the question was:

One of my ongoing patients? It *has* happened. I would stay on the phone as long as it takes. If they are deadly serious, with a gun in their hand, threatening to blow their head off, I might ask them if they think it would be helpful for us to meet; that would simply be moving to another location, as it were, the kind of inconvenience that the patient is introducing anyway! There are times when such therapeutic actions are necessary. That offer in itself is so powerful and significant that it can rattle the patient and create a situation of hope, and diminish the anger, the revenge fantasies etc. Secondly, if they are being obnoxious, I would ask them if they would object to giving me names or telephone numbers of relatives who I might call to help them. If they don't want to do that, then I would have to resort to other measures. I would say: 'You know, by calling me you have given me responsibility for what happens, so I am now going to call the police and make sure that they protect you and take you to hospital'. So it may be anything from calling the police to seeing them in person. If somebody is in bad trouble, there is no reason for not seeing them, even if it is at an odd hour of the day (or night). Other specialists, internists, gynecologists, do! (Cited in Hellinga et al., 2000, p. 40)

The important thing to keep in mind is that a patient who is calling with a gun pointed to his temple is not one person. He is split into two parts: one who is holding the gun and the other who is going to be killed. And, since there are 'two people' on the phone, the therapist must listen and talk to both of them. His approach must oscillate between empathy and reality confrontation. This is even more important when the patient is calling from an unknown location and is unwilling to reveal where he or she is at.[39] Moving between empathic 'affirmative interventions' (Killingmo, 1989), e.g. 'I know you are in severe pain', 'I can see why the thought of killing yourself would occur you in this situation', and interpretive reminders that the patient's calling in itself indicates that he still has hopes from the therapist, would calm down the patient some. And then the therapist can either ask the patient to go to the hospital or even meet him somewhere *midway* (to emphasize the mutuality of their work) between the therapist's residence and the patient's location at that time. It is a matter of tact, an admixture of kindness and limit-setting, and above all, of keeping the patient out of harm's way through providing one's unerring concern as the temporary safety-net for him.

THE AFTERMATH OF A COMPLETED SUICIDE

Clinical work with suicidal patients does not come to an end if they succeed in committing suicide. The aftermath of the tragedy poses its own challenges. It presents the clinician with 'conflicting tensions between maintaining patient confidentiality, providing support to the suicide survivors, and implementing risk management principles that limit liability exposure' (Simon, 2004, p. 191). It should be remembered that the duty to maintain confidentiality of the patient's records follows the patient in death, unless a specific court decision or statute in a particular jurisdiction indicates otherwise. As a general rule, therefore, written authorization from the executor of the patient's will should be obtained before releasing the patient's medical records. In unclear situations, legal counsel should be sought.

Besides such medico-legal concerns (Simon 2004, pp. 195-221), there is the issue of dealing with the family members. The therapist must not refuse to meet them, unless they are bringing a legal charge against him. As far as possible, he should provide factual answers to their questions without revealing too many painful details of the patient's inner life. The immediate priority should be to console the family, witness their grief, and empathize with their sense of loss. At times, arranging ongoing care for one or more of the survivors might also be indicated.

However, such outward focus must not lead to ignoring that a patient's suicide can have serious effects upon the therapist himself. Feelings of guilt, shame, anger, and doubts about one's professional competence are common under such circumstances (Gitlin, 1999; Hendin et al., 2000). Mourning reactions can be protracted and alter one's views about life in general and the psychotherapeutic enterprise in particular. Foster (1987), an analyst who lost two patients to suicide in succession, captures this anguish well:

> In an odd way, I went to sleep, a sleep that lasted several months. I didn't feel it connected to the suicides. It just seemed I was fatigued, and understandably so because I was overworked. I didn't feel like entertaining or being entertained. It was as if I was sleepwalking and, in that state, I made it possible for myself to

heal. And heal I did, though things are never quite the same. Psychiatry deals mainly with life, and rarely with death and dying. When patients used to ask me, what will you do if I kill myself, I used to reply something to the effect that they would not be around to see it, but that after their burial things would go on more or less as they had been, though they wouldn't be the same. Now I keep silent. I dislike platitudes, especially my own... I have grown to respect my patients' freedom differently and to be keenly aware of my limitations. (pp. 202, 204)

Much intrapsychic work, it seems, needs to happen to come out of such mourning. Whether the therapist can do such work on his or her own or would need professional help is an open question that needs to be tackled in each individual circumstance of this sort. It is useful to remember in this context that the Clinician Task Force of the American Association of Suicidology offers a number of resources to therapists who have had patients commit suicide.[40]

CONCLUDING REMARKS

In this chapter, I have attempted a broad survey of issues pertaining to suicide. I have presented some epidemiological data which prepares one to detect patterns of vulnerability in this realm. Following this, I have elucidated the psychodynamic underpinnings of suicide, including the disheartened, angry, guilt-ridden, and narcissistic motives behind such an act. I have then discussed the assessment of suicide risk, noting the complexities and shortcomings of this enterprise. Management-wise, I have noted the role of the therapist's holding functions, limit-setting and interpreting, utilizing adjunct measures (e.g. family meetings, medications, and hospitalization), and managing countertransference difficulties that often crop up in dealing with chronically self-destructive individuals.

Throughout all this, my perspective has been biopsychosocial and multifactorial vis-à-vis both the etiology and treatment of suicidal tendencies. In the latter realm especially, the reader would have discerned a certain tension between two polarities. This tension results from the fact that technical approaches derived from the 'classic' and the 'romantic' visions of psychoanalysis (Strenger, 1989) differ considerably from each other. The former are inherent in the technical stances of Kernberg (1975, 1984) and the latter in those of Winnicott (1960) and Adler (1985) cited above. The former involves a firm, confrontational, limit-setting and interpretive approach, and the latter involves a flexible, holding, supportive and affirmative approach. The former holds the patient responsible for controlling his suicidal impulses while outside the sessions and seeking help if such impulses seem to be getting out of control. The latter says that the therapist should be available on a twenty-four hour basis to the patient during the times of crisis. The advantage of the former approach is that it allows for the full development (and, therefore a deeper interpretation) of the negative transference which the suicidal patient needs to experience. The advantage of the latter approach is that it provides auxiliary support for ego functions that the patient is, for the time being, incapable of; it therefore offers the hope of strengthening the patient's ego over time. The risk of the former approach is that the patient can feel rejected and even 'punished' for his suicidal impulses. The risk of the latter is that the patient can become infantilized and addicted to the therapist. All in all, therefore, an exclusive use of one or the other approach seems less useful than an informed, judicious, and empathically attuned oscillation between them (Akhtar, 1992, 2000).

Even such broadening of perspective does not exhaust what therapists dealing with suicidal individuals need to keep in mind. They must not forget that the majority of mentally ill people do not kill themselves and that many who do might not meet the criteria for diagnosable mental illness. They must keep in mind that committing suicide is not the fate of the dregs of society, but also of a large number of accomplished individuals ranging from Vincent van Gogh to Virginia Woolf, from Pyotr Tchaikovsky to Kurt Cobain, from Ernest Hemingway to Primo Levi, and from Sylvia Plath to Abbie Hoffman. Also to be remembered is the fact that situations might exist where 'physician-assisted suicide' might not be entirely irrational: Freud's death by a morphine injection given by his physician, Max Schur, when he was old and suffering from severe neoplasm-related pain, is an example of this. Indeed many nations (most prominently, The Netherlands) are developing constitutional guidelines for the individual's right to decide upon such life and death matters. Therapists dealing with suicidal individuals must not overlook that when all is said and done, the patient's life (and death) belongs only to the patient. And, this brings us to Albert Camus' (1942) resounding declaration that: 'there is but one truly philosophical problem, and that is suicide. Judging whether life is or is not worth living amounts to answering the fundamental question of philosophy.'

NOTES

1   Two comments need to be added here. One is in the nature of acknowledgment and the other involves a clarification. The first pertains to the
fact that the idea of conducting the initial evaluation on consecutive
days (instead of weekly appointments) was suggested to me by my
good friend, Philadelphia-based psychoanalyst Albert Kaplan, some
fifteen years ago. Having found the practice extremely useful, I have
stuck with it and, of course, remain thankful to Dr. Kaplan. The second
point I want to make pertains to patients arriving for a consultation
from out of town. To them, I generally recommend two sessions of one
and a half hour length, separated by a hour interval, in the same day.
This avoids the necessity of an overnight stay in town and therefore
saves the patient extra expense. Occasionally, however, more time than
this might be needed and an overnight stay in a nearby hotel becomes
inevitable.

2   The clinical material offered in this chapter and indeed throughout this
book makes use of fictitious names. I have opted to use names instead
of the conventional initials which appear too 'dry' and, frankly, not
quite human to me. I have also made great effort to disguise the identi-
ties of the individuals involved without the sacrifice of clinical accuracy.

3   Highly pertinent in this context is the observation made by Professor
A.K. Agarwal of Lucknow, India, that the customary mental status ex-
amination is useful with psychiatric inpatients but has little applicability to non-psychotic, outpatient populations (Rajnish Mago, personal
communication, October 9, 2007).

4   Attempts at distinguishing neurotic ('oedipal') from borderline ('preoedipal') character organizations must be tempered by the fact that the
two frequently overlap and coexist. They might be condensed into
each other or one might serve as a defense against the emergence of
the other. Oedipal wishes are often associated with preoedipal fears
(e.g., separation and loss) and preoedipal object hunger frequently

143

takes on a triangular and sexualized flavor. Oedipal drive derivatives can camouflage unresolved symbiotic longings and a preoedipal baby-like pleading can be a regressive refuge from the guilt and anxiety of oedipal competitiveness. All in all, there is much fluidity between what are generally regarded as categorically neurotic and borderline organizations.

5   A curious note to the literature on psychological-mindedness was added by Werman (1979) who noted that this capacity is not only evident in the ability for self observation but also in one's view of the external world. Exploration of the latter aspect however is often neglected. Werman observed that the inability to accept random occurrences and intolerance of ambiguity in the external world are often the outward manifestation of poor psychological-mindedness. The ability to believe in chance and to tolerate uncertainty are consequences of the development of secondary process thinking and may be regarded as a specialized aspects of reality-testing.

6   A simple and short question about the role of animals in the patient's life, asked during the initial evaluation, can often reveal clinically significant information.

7   This emphasis upon the therapist's activities does not eliminate the fact that the patient also assesses the therapist during the initial evaluation. Such assessment, I believe, consists of the patient's looking for the qualities of affinity, empathy, kindness, patience, knowledge, and competence. The patient wishes to be understood and feel that the therapist can help him.

8   Such luxury of ethics is generally out of the reach of trainees who are assigned cases and have little say in selecting patients. The availability of supervision, however, provides a balancing reassurance in this context. Greater responsibility rests with psychotherapists who, while otherwise experienced, might not be competent to treat this or that type of patient for a variety of reasons.

9   Supervision is another area where boundary violations tend to take place. Haesler (1993) has elucidated the importance of adequate distance in the supervisor-supervisee relationship and Gabbard & Lester (1995) as well as Celenza (2007) have discussed the vicissitudes of boundary violations in the context of psychotherapy or psychoanalytic supervision in useful detail.

10   Parens (2006) has astutely noted that models based upon attachment (Bowlby, 1969, 1973) and systems theory (Sander, 1964, 1983) do not start from an assumed self-object unity but from an assumed dyad. The tension that exists between them and the 'dual unity' models (e.g. Mahler's and Winnicott's) has to be accepted as such.

11   For a detailed account of boundary violations during the early days of psychoanalysis, including the egregious acts of some 'pioneers', see Gabbard and Lester (1995, pp. 68-86).

12   This is not to say that patients do not violate the therapeutic frame by themselves. The fact is that patients with impulse-ridden character pathology chronically test the boundaries of treatment (e.g. lateness, missed sessions, delayed payments). Even in the absence of severe personality dysfunction, major transference regressions can lead to enactments that defy all agreed-upon limits and guidelines of the treatment (see Brenner, 2006; Kogan, 2006). These patient-initiated violations constitute a counterpart to those committed by predatory therapists. Together these two types of transgressions account for the minority of boundary violations, most of which are 'co-created' in the intersubjective crucible of transference-countertransference phenomena.

13   It is always helpful if the therapist familiarizes himself with the sociocultural and ethnic background of the patient. Acquiring 'anthropological knowledge of culture' (e.g. lay of the land, demography, religious festivals) is good but not a substitute for 'psychoanalytic knowledge of culture' (e.g. myths, prevalent fantasies, desirable roles). A therapist equipped with both these types of knowledge of the patient's culture is in a far better position to understand him than one who lacks such knowledge (Sudhir Kakar, personal communication, November 11, 2007).

14   Sadly, even the founder of psychoanalysis, Sigmund Freud, was not immune to such temptations. In a behavior characterized as 'reprehensible' by Gabbard and Lester (1995, p. 83), he encouraged one of his patients, Horace Frink, to divorce his wife, marry the wealthy woman he was having an affair with, and donate a large sum of money thus acquired to the Psychoanalytic Funds.

15   Such guidelines are generally sufficient for most patients. However, for severe borderline patients who present with marked impulsivity and grossly disorganized lives, a more structured 'initial contract' (Kernberg et al., 1990; Selzer, 1987) might be required.

16   Physical contact between therapist and patient is a matter riddled with conceptual, technical, ethical, and moral difficulties. On the one hand, the risks involved are great and it is advisable to avoid such contact and handle the patient's desire for it by exploration, interpretation, and reconstruction. On the other hand, a handshake at the initial encounter or a gentle hug at termination might not be entirely inappropriate, especially if the therapist is well-intentioned and the patient's ego functioning is intact. For more details on therapist-patient physical contact, see the special issue of *Psychoanalytic Inquiry* (volume 20) which contains some very good papers on this topic.

[17] As a young psychiatric resident some thirty-five years ago, I once asked my supervisor, Daniel Josephthal, if he ever experienced sexual feelings towards his patients. A consummate analyst and a *mensch* to boot, he responded by saying: 'Why? Do you think I am made of stone?' His response did wonders for my then harsh superego and inexperienced work-ego.

[18] For a different slant on the conceptual interaction between money and psychoanalysis, see *The Psychology of Investing* by Lawrence Lifson and Richard Geist (1999).

[19] Individual psychology is not the sole determinant of this type of behavior. Cultural factors also play an important role in mobilizing and reinforcing the fantasy that material acquisition can bring happiness (Benson, 2000). Indeed, a deliberately engineered elevation of human wishes into 'needs' (see Akhtar, 2000, for the need-wish distinction) is a typical maneuver of capitalism which uses advertising as its slave for this purpose. To meet these needs, one requires money which, in turn, becomes emotionally exalted. It is hardly surprising then that in a country that prides itself on the separation between church and state, the one place where God is explicitly endorsed is upon its dollar bill!

[20] A two page section in Fenichel's (1945) encyclopedic compendium of early psychoanalytic literature and Bergler's (1971) monograph on the topic notwithstanding, the fact is that psychoanalysis makes little reference to gambling. It is popular literature that captures the subjective trials and tribulations of the gambler in its minutest details (see especially Alvarez, 1983, and McMannus, 2003). Knapp (2000) has collected portrayals of the gambler's inner experience by some of the world's greatest authors (e.g. Balzac, Poe, Dostoevsky and Hesse) in an elegant volume.

[21] An interesting dilemma for the senior clinician at this point involves the choice between referring the patient to someone with less experience who can see him more frequently at what he can pay or seeing the patient oneself but at a lesser frequency. No hard and fast rules can be set to deal with this dilemma but, with unusually difficult cases, the latter option often makes more sense (Klauber, 1981).

[22] The section titled 'judiciously accommodating the therapeutic frame to the patients' cultural attitudes' in my book on immigration (Akhtar, 1999) addresses these very types of issues.

[23] The situation is, however, more complicated in the case of children and adolescents. Dependent upon their parents for transportation and money, they can hardly be held responsible for fee negotiation, delayed payments, and missed sessions. Parents, especially if they are at war with each other, tend to act out all sorts of issues that affect the course of their child's treatment, including the payment for it. Not infrequently, this puts the child therapist in an ethical dilemma where the choice

is to continue treating the child without adequate or no compensation, or to disrupt the case of a truly helpless being who has little knowledge or control over the financial matters involved.

24 It was long after having written this passage that I came across a similar discussion (Schlesinger, 2003) of why charging money for missed sessions is not a good practice. I urge the reader to look at this far more erudite defense of the position I've taken here.

25 Imagine an unaffected New Orleans therapist charging his patient for missing his session during the Katrina crisis and you will get the point I am trying to make here.

26 Time is another out-of-control variable in the lives of these patients. Dependent upon public transport and lacking coverage for children at home makes it difficult for them to be punctual for clinical appointments. These realities are also exploited by characterological, neurotic, and transference-based agendas. The resulting lateness is hardly responsive to interpretive approaches; the patient feels misunderstood. It seems puzzling to him that the therapist is showing great interest in his five minute delay rather than in his keeping the appointment at all. See Lager & Zwerling (1980), Akhtar (1999), for further details on this matter.

27 Altman (1993) questions such 'two-tiered psychoanalysis' (p. 47) proposing that the variables of ego strength, verbal intelligence, and capacity to tolerate the therapist abstinence are themselves products of a Calvinist cultural bias. He suggests that psychoanalytic therapies based upon the object-relations model (Fairbairn, 1952) are more effective with clinic patients than those derived from the classical ego-psychological approach.

28 The Berlin Psychoanalytic Clinic was the first such service to be established. It opened in February 1920 and was followed by the Viennese Psychoanalytic Ambulatorium in 1922 and London Clinic of Psychoanalysis on Freud's 70th birthday in 1926. The first psychoanalytic clinic providing low-fee and sometimes free treatment in the United States opened at the State University Medical Center in New York in 1950. Over the subsequent years, it became customary for psychoanalytic institutes to make low-fee and free treatment available through their candidates training. This practice persists.

29 Some creative patients might compensate for their low fee by giving a painting or sculpture to the therapist. Others might want to rely exclusively upon such a barter system, i.e. always giving things instead of money. And, there might be regions in the world where such exchange might be quite acceptable. Within our own culture, however, this matter remains far from simple. One is better in erring on the side of caution or, at least, consulting a reliable colleague before entering into such an arrangement.

30   I do not charge money for a brief initial consultation to medical students, physicians, applicants for psychoanalytic training and immigrants from India and their offspring.

31   *Purchase of Friendship*, the cynical subtitle of William Schofield's (1964) book on psychotherapy, might finally find an apt use in such circumstances.

32   'Bridging interventions' (Kernberg, 1975) denote those remarks of the analyst which emanate from his or her capacity to retain a patient's split and contradictory self and object-representations in mind (since the patient has a tendency to 'forget' affectively one or the other extreme of his experience). The aim of such interventions is to undo the psychic compartmentalization caused by splitting. In elaborating Kernberg's views, Akhtar (1995, 1998) notes that 'bridging interventions' involve the therapist's display—by gentle verbal reminders or a subtle shift in the tone of voice—that he at least has not 'forgotten' the transference configuration that is opposite to the one currently active. Thus the therapist might make a mild, en passant remark during the course of a lengthier intervention about the patient's hostility when the latter is being too idealizing, or about love when the patient is being too demeaning.

33   This is not to say that more aggressive interventions might not be needed with patients whose stalking patterns are more aggressive and overtly hostile. These measures might include limit-setting, obtaining written contracts, seeking legal advice, and even informing the police. (For more details on the management of such patients, see Lion & Herschler, 1998, and Mullen & Purcell, 2007).

34   This requires discipline. In clinics where people constantly pass by one's door and, seeing it open, suddenly feel the need to ask all sorts of questions, this might be especially difficult. With practice, however, one becomes proficient in it and others also begin to respect the boundaries thus created.

35   Addressing the patient by first name has become a widely accepted practice now. I, however, consider this appropriate only under three circumstances: (i) when the patient is a child or an adolescent; (ii) when the patient is a state of 'emotional flooding' (Volkan, 1976; Akhtar, 1995) regardless of whether this involves rage, sadness, or fear; and (iii) when the therapist is making a reconstruction that envisions the patient as a child.

36   Another arena in which oscillation between homeostatic and disruptive attunement has salutary effects is that of teaching. A good teacher tells the students what they already know and thus generates a feeling of self-worth and confidence in them (homeostatic attunement). Then, in a swift movement, the teacher presents new information to them,

challenging and expanding their intellectual horizons (disruptive attunement). More importantly, a good teacher is the one who enjoys his work and knows the velocity and intensity of such oscillations suitable for his students.

[37]   Conversely, many individuals who are unconsciously seeking death do not make overt suicidal gestures. They might destroy themselves via slow, subtle, and chronic self-harming acts (e.g. smoking, excessive drinking, neglected health care) or ones that are abrupt and sudden (e.g. provoked homicides, unconsciously engineered accidents). It is for such tendencies that the term 'parasuicide' or 'sub-meditated death' (Farberow & Shneidman, 1971) has been coined.

[38]   Even though the emphasis in explaining the patient's diagnosis should be upon the patient's subjective experience, there is no reason to avoid the 'official' diagnostic terminology under such circumstances. The recommendation of some material for the family to read (e.g. pertinent pages from DSM-IV, 1990) can also be helpful.

[39]   A situation that may occur once in a lifetime involves receiving such a phone call at home while one is having company for dinner or, say, a Sunday afternoon barbecue. While no hard and fast rules can be set, keeping the following guidelines in mind might help: (i) emotionally give up on the party; you may or may not be able to return to it but at least for the time being you have to renounce the pleasure of participating in it; (ii) tell a trusted individual (e.g. spouse, live-in partner, friend) that you have to handle a clinical emergency; (iii) request him or her to take care of your guests and, of course, inform him where the food and drinks are; (iv) go to a quiet part of the house where you can talk with the patient without disruption; (v) mentally prepare yourself to spend anywhere between a few minutes to a few hours on the situation; (vi) keep the usual 'good cop-bad cop' strategy used by the police in handling hostage situations in mind; you will need it since both empathic and limit-setting measures would be warranted in this conversation; and (vii) be prepared to meet the patient half way, in an open, well-lit public space, should he be willing to hand over the gun only to you.

[40]   See: http://www.suicidology.org/web/guest/clinicians   (accessed February, 2008).

References

Abraham, K. (1917). The spending of money in anxiety states. In: *Selected Papers of Karl Abraham, M.D.*, pp. 299-302. New York: Brunner/Mazel, 1965.

Abraham, K. (1924). Manic depressive states and the pre-genital levels of the libido. In: *Selected Papers of Karl Abraham*, pp. 418-478. New York: Brunner/Mazel, 1980.

Adler, G. (1981). The borderline-narcissistic personality disorders continue on. *American Journal of Psychiatry* 138:46-50.

Adler, G. (1985). *Borderline Psychopathology and Its Treatment*. New York: Jason Aronson.

Adler, J. (2005). In search of the spiritual. *Newsweek*, pp. 46-64, September 5, 2005.

Akhtar, S. (1984). The syndrome of identity diffusion. *American Journal of Psychiatry* 141:1381-1835.

Akhtar, S. (1990). Concept of interpersonal distance in borderline personality disorder (letter to the editor). *American Journal of Psychiatry* 147:1061-1062.

Akhtar, S. (1991). Three fantasies related to unresolved separation-individuation: a less recognized aspect of severe character pathology. In: *Beyond the Symbiotic Orbit: Advances in Separation-Individuation Theory*, eds. S. Akhtar and H. Parens, pp. 261-284. Hillsdale, NJ: The Analytic Press.

Akhtar, S. (1992a). *Broken Structures: Severe Personality Disorders and Their Treatment*. Northvale, NJ: Jason Aronson.

150

Akhtar, S. (1992b). Tethers, orbits, and invisible fences: clinical, developmental, sociocultural, and technical aspects of optimal distance. In: *When the Body Speaks: Psychological Meanings in Kinetic Clues*, eds. S. Kramer and S. Akhtar, pp. 21-57. Northvale, NJ: Jason Aronson.

Akhtar, S. (1994). Object constancy and adult psychopathology. *International Journal of Psychoanalysis* 75:441-455.

Akhtar, S. (1995). *Quest for Answers: Understanding and Treating Severe Personality Disorders*. Northvale, NJ: Jason Aronson.

Akhtar, S. (1996). 'Someday...' and 'if only...' fantasies: pathological optimism and inordinate nostalgia as related forms of idealization. *Journal of the American Psychoanalytic Association* 44:723-753.

Akhtar, S. (1997). Constitution, environment, and fantasy in the organization of the psychotic core. In: *The Seed of Madness: Constitution, Environment, and Fantasy in the Organization of the Psychotic Core*, eds. V.D. Volkan and S. Akhtar, pp. 179-201. Madison, CT: International Universities Press.

Akhtar, S. (1998). From simplicity through contradiction to paradox: the evolving psychic reality of the borderline patient in treatment. *International Journal of Psychoanalysis* 79:241-252.

Akhtar, S. (1999). *Immigration and Identity: Turmoil, Treatment, and Transformation*. Northvale, NJ: Jason Aronson.

Akhtar, S. (2000). Mental pain and the cultural ointment of poetry. *International Journal of Psychoanalysis* 81:229-244.

Akhtar, S. (2006a). *Interpersonal Boundaries: Variations and Violations*. Lanham, MD: Jason Aronson.

Akhtar, S. (2006b). Experiencing oneness: pathological pursuit or normal necessity? Discussion of Kogan's chapter: breaking of boundaries and craving for oneness. In: *Interpersonal Boundaries: Variations and Violations*, ed. S. Akhtar, pp. 87-97. Lanham, MD: Jason Aronson.

Akhtar, S. (2007). From unmentalized xenophobia to messianic sadism: some reflections on the phenomenology of prejudice. In: *The Future of Prejudice: Psychoanalysis and the Prevention of Prejudice*, eds. H. Parens, A. Mahfouz, S. W. Twemlow, and D.E. Scharff, pp. 7-19. Landham, MD: Jason Aronson.

Akhtar, S. & Kramer, S. (1999). Beyond the parental orbit: brothers, sisters, and others. In: *Brothers and Sisters: Developmental, Dy-*

namic, and Technical Aspects of the Sibling Relationship, ed. S. Akhtar and S. Kramer, pp. 1-24. Northvale, NJ: Jason Aronson.

Altman, N. (1993). Psychoanalysis and the urban poor. *Psychoanalytic Dialogues* 3:29-49.

Alvarez, A. (1983). *The Biggest Game in Town*. San Francisco, CA: Chronicle Books.

American Psychiatric Association (2003). Practice guidelines for the assessment and treatment of patients with suicidal behaviors. *American Journal of Psychiatry* 160 (suppl.):1-60.

Anzieu, D. (1990). *Psychic Envelopes*. London: Karnac Books.

Anzieu, D. (1992). The sound image of the self. *International Review of Psychoanalysis* 6:23-32.

Appelbaum, S.A. (1973). Psychological mindedness: word, concept, and essence. *International Journal of Psychoanalysis* 54:35-46.

Armstrong, P.S. (2000). *Opening Gambits: The First Session of Psychotherapy*. Northvale, NJ: Jason Aronson.

Asch, S. (1976). Varieties of negative therapeutic reaction and problems of technique. *Journal of the American Psychoanalytic Association* 24:383-407.

Bachrach, H. & Leaff, L. (1978). Analyzability: a systematic review of the clinical quantitative literature. *Journal of the American Psychoanalytic Association* 26:881-920.

Balint, M. (1959). *Thrills and Regressions*. London: Hogarth Press.

Balint, M. (1968). *The Basic Fault*. London: Tavistock.

Balsam, R. (1984). A special transference: the perfect patient. *Psychoanalytic Study of the Child* 39:285-300.

Bellak, L. & Faithorn, P.E. (1981). *Crises and Special Problems in Psychoanalysis and Psychotherapy*. New York: Brunnel/Mazel.

Benson, A.L. (2000). *I Shop Therefore I Am: Compulsive Buying and the Search for Self*. Northvale, NJ: Jason Aronson.

Bergler, E. (1947). The psychopathology of bargain hunters. *Journal of Clinical Psychology* 8:623-627.

Bergler, E. (1971). *The Psychology of Gambling*. New York: International Universities Press.

Bergman, A. (1980). Ours, yours, mine. In: *Rapprochement: The Critical Subphase of Separation-Individuation*, eds. R.F. Lax, S. Bach, and J.A. Burland, pp. 199-216. New York: Jason Aronson.

Bernfeld, S. (1929). Selbstomord. *Zeitschrift fur Psychoanalytische Padagogik* 3:353-363.

Bick, E. (1968). The experience of the skin in early object-relations. *International Journal of Psychoanalysis* 49:484-486.

Bion, W.R. (1959). Attacks on linking. *International Journal of Psychoanalysis* 40:308-315.

Bion, W.R. (1967). *Second Thoughts*. London: Heinemann.

Blanton, S. (1976). The hidden faces of money. In: *The Psychoanalysis of Money*, ed. E. Borneman, pp. 253-270. New York: Urizen Books.

Blos, P. (1967). The second individuation process of adolescence. *Psychoanalytic Study of the Child* 22:162-186.

Blum, H .P. (1973). The concept of erotized transference. *Journal of the American Psychoanalytic Association* 21:61-76.

Bonovitz, J. (1998). Reflections of the self in the cultural looking glass. In: *The Colors of Childhood: Separation-Individuation Across Cultural, Racial, and Ethnic Differences*, eds. S. Akhtar and S. Kramer, pp. 169-198. Northvale, NJ: Jason Aronson.

Bonovitz, J. (2007). The self and its boundaries: an introductory overview. In: *Interpersonal Boundaries: Variations and Violations*, ed. S. Akhtar, pp. 1-14. Lanham, MD: Jason Aronson.

Boris, H. (1976). On hope: its nature and psychotherapy. *International Review of Psychoanalysis* 3:139-150.

Borneman, E. (1976). *The Psychoanalysis of Money*. New York: Urizen Books.

Bouvet, M. (1958). Technical variation and the concept of distance. *International Journal of Psychoanalysis* 39:211-221.

Bowlby, J. (1969). *Attachment and Loss: Volume I: Attachment*. New York: Basic Books.

Bowlby, J. (1973). *Attachment and Loss: Volume II: Separation*. New York: Basic Books.

Brenner, C. (1979). Working alliance, therapeutic alliance, and transference. *Journal of the American Psychoanalytic Association* 27:137-145.

Brenner, I. (1994). The dissociative character: a reconsideration of 'multiple personality'. *Journal of the American Psychoanalytic Association* 42:819-846.

Brenner, I. (2001). *Dissociation of Trauma: Theory, Phenomenology, and Technique*. Madison, CT: International Universities Press.

Brenner, I. (2006). Going over the edge—a one-person or two person psychology? Discussion of Gabbard's chapter, 'sexual and nonsexual boundary violations in psychoanalysis and psychotherapy'. In: *Interpersonal Boundaries: Variations and Violations*, ed. S. Akhtar, pp. 49-59. Lanham, MD: Jason Aronson.

Bruch, H. (1974). *Learning Psychotherapy: Rationale and Ground Rules.* Cambridge, MA : Harvard University Press.

Burnham, D.L., Gladstone, A.E., & Gibson, R.W. (1969). *Schizophrenia and the Need-Fear Dilemma.* New York: International Universities Press.

Busch, K.A., Clark, D.C., Fawcett, J., et al (1993). Clinical features of inpatient suicide. *Psychiatric Annals* 23:256-262.

Bush, K.A. & Fawcett, J. (2004). A fine-grained study of inpatients who commit suicide. *Psychiatric Annals* 34: 357-364.

Camus, A. (1942). *The Myth of Sisyphus*, trans. J. O'Brien. New York: Alfred A. Knopf, Inc., 1955.

Carstairs, G.M. (1957). *The Twice Born: A Study of a Community of High-Caste Hindus.* Bloomington, IN: Indiana University Press.

Casement, P. (1982). Some pressures on the analyst for physical contact during the re-living of an early trauma. *International Review of Psychoanalysis* 9:279-286.

Celenza, A. (2007). *Sexual Boundary Violations: Therapeutic, Supervisory, and Academic Contexts.* Lanham, MD: Jason Aronson.

Chodoff, P. (1986). The effect of third-party payment on the practice of psychotherapy. In: *The Last Taboo: Money as Symbol and Reality in Psychotherapy and Psychoanalysis*, ed. D.W. Krueger, pp. 111-120. New York: Brunner/Mazel.

Coen, S. (2002). *Affect Intolerance in Analyst and Patient.* Northvale, NJ: Jason Aronson.

Colby, K.M. (1951). *A Primer for Psychotherapists.* New York: The Ronald Press Company.

Coltart, N. (1988). The assessment of psychological-mindedness in the diagnostic interview. *British Journal of Psychiatry* 153:819-820.

Deutsch, H. (1942). Such forms of emotional disturbance and their relationship to schizophrenia. *Psychiatric Quarterly* 11:301-321.

Diagnostic and Statistical Manual of Mental Disorders—IV (1990). Washington, DC: American Psychiatric Association.

Dublin, L.I. (1963). *Suicide: A Sociological and Statistical Study.* New York: Ronald Press.

Eidelberg, L. (1968). *Encyclopedia of Psychoanalysis.* New York: The Free Press.

Eissler, K.R. (1949). Some problems of delinquency. In: *Searchlights on Delinquency*, ed. K.R. Eissler, pp. 3-25. New York: International Universities Press.

Erikson, E. (1950). *Childhood and Society*. New York: W.W. Norton.

Erikson, E. (1959). *Identity and the Life Cycle*. New York: International Universities Press.

Esman, A.H. (1983). The 'stimulus barrier': review and consideration. *Psychoanalytic Study of the Child* 38:193-217.

Fairbairn, W.R.D. (1952). *An Object Relations Theory of the Personality*. New York: Basic Books.

Fareberow, N.L. & Shneidman, E.S. (1961). *The Cry for Help*. New York: McGraw-Hill.

Fawcett, J. (2001). Treating impulsivity and anxiety in the suicidal patient. *Annals of the New York Academy of Science* 932:94-105.

Federn, P. (1952). *Ego Psychology and the Psychoses*. New York: Basic Books.

Fenichel, O. (1938). The drive to amass wealth. *Psychoanalytic Quarterly* 7:69-95.

Fenichel, O. (1945). *The Psychoanalytic Theory of Neurosis*. New York: W.W. Norton.

Ferenczi, S. (1914). The ontogenesis of the interest in money. In: *First Contributions to Psychoanalysis*, pp. 319-331. New York: Brunner/Mazel, 1980.

Ferenczi, S. (1929). The unwelcome child and his death instinct. In: *Final Contributions to the Problems of Methods of Psychoanalysis*, pp.102-107. New York: Brunner/Mazel.

Foster, B. (1987). Suicide and the impact on the therapist. In: *Attachment and the Therapeutic Process: Essays in Honor of Otto Alan Will, Jr.* Eds. J.L. Sacksteder, D.P. Schwartz, and Y. Akabane, pp. 197-204. Madison, CT: International Universities Press.

Freeman, D. (1998). Emotional refueling in development, mythology, and cosmology: the Japanese separation-individuation experience. In: *The Colors of Childhood: Separation-Individuation Across Cultural, Racial, and Ethnic Differences*, eds. S. Akhtar and S. Kramer, pp. 17-60. Northvale, NJ: Jason Aronson.

Freud, A. (1922) Beating fantasies and daydreams. *International Journal of Psychoanalysis* 4:89-100.

Freud, A. (1936). The ego and the mechanisms of defense. In: *The Writings of Anna Freud, Vol. II*, pp. New York: International Universities Press, 1966.

Freud, S. (1895). Project for a scientific psychology. *Standard Edition* 1:283-398.

Freud, S. (1900). Interpretation of dreams. *Standard Edition* 4:1-337.

Freud, S. (1908). Character and anal erotism. *Standard Edition* 9:167-176.

Freud, S. (1910). Contributions to a discussion on suicide. *Standard Edition* 11:231-232.

Freud, S. (1913). On beginning the treatment. *Standard Edition* 12:123-144.

Freud, S. (1915). Observations on transference love. *Standard Edition* 12:159-171.

Freud, S. (1916). Some character types met with in psychoanalytic work. *Standard Edition* 14:310-333.

Freud, S. (1917). Mourning and melancholia. *Standard Edition* 14:237-260.

Freud, S. (1920). Beyond the pleasure principle. *Standard Edition* 18:7-64.

Freud, S. (1923). The ego and the id. *Standard Edition* 17:3-68.

Freud, S. (1924). The economic problem of masochism. *Standard Edition* 19:155-170.

Freud, S. (1925). Some psychical consequences of the anatomical distinction between the sexes. *Standard Edition* 19:241-258.

Frosch, J. (1988a). Psychotic character versus borderline: part I. *International Journal of Psychoanalysis* 69:347-365.

Frosch, J. (1988b). Psychotic character versus borderline: part II. *International Journal of Psychoanalysis* 69:445-460.

Fuqua, P.B. (1986). Classical psychoanalytic views of money. In: *The Last Taboo: Money as Symbol and Reality in Psychotherapy and Psychoanalysis*, ed. D.W. Krueger, pp. 17-23. New York: Brunner/Mazel.

Gabbard, G.O. (1997). Challenges in the analysis of adult patients with histories of childhood sexual abuse. *Canadian Journal of Psychoanalysis* 5:1-25.

Gabbard, G.O. (2006). Sexual and nonsexual boundary violations in psychoanalysis and psychotherapy. In: *Interpersonal Bound-*

aries: Variations and Violations, ed. S. Akhtar, pp. 39-48. Lanham, MD: Jason Aronson.

Gabbard, G.O. & Lester, E. P (1995). *Boundaries and Boundary Violations in Psychoanalysis*. New York: Basic Books.

Garfield, R. (2007). Clinical perspectives on the development of boundaries: discussion of Tyson's chapter, 'Boundary formation in children: normality and pathology'. In: *Interpersonal Boundaries: Variations and Violations*, ed. S. Akhtar, pp. 29-46. Lanham, MD: Jason Aronson.

Gediman, H. (1971). The concept of stimulus barrier. *International Journal of Psychoanalysis* 52:243-255.

Gill, M. & Redlich, F. (1954). *Initial Interview in Psychiatric Practice*. New York: International Universities Press.

Gitlin, M.J. (1999). A psychiatrist's reaction to a patient's suicide. *American Journal of Psychiatry* 156:1630-1634.

Goldberg, A. (1987). The place of apology in psychoanalysis and psychotherapy. *International Review of Psychoanalysis* 14:409-422.

Gorton. G. & Akhtar, S. (1990). The literature of personality disorders—1985-88: trends, issues, and controversies. *Hospital and Community Psychiatry* 41:39-51.

Greenson, R. (1965). The working alliance and the transference neurosis. Psychoanalytic Quarterly 34:155-181.

Greenson, R.R. (1965). The working alliance and the transference neurosis. *Psychoanalytic Quarterly* 34:155-175.

Greenspan, S. (1977). The oedipal-preoedipal dilemma: a reformulation in the light of object relations theory. *International Review of Psychoanalysis* 4:381-391.

Grinker, R. & Werble, B. (1977). *The Borderline Patient*. New York: Jason Aronson.

Gruenert, U. (1979). The negative therapeutic reaction as a reactivation of a disturbed process of separation in the transference. *Bulletin of the European Psychoanalytical Federation* 16:5-9.

Gunderson, J. (1985). *Borderline Personality Disorder*. Washington, D.C.: American Psychiatric Press.

Guntrip, H. (1969). *Schizoid Phenomena, Object Relations, and the Self*. New York: International Universities Press.

Haesler, L. (1993). Adequate distance in the relationship between supervisor and supervisee. *International Journal of Psychoanalysis* 74:547-555.

Hall, R.C., Platt, D.E., & Hall, R.C. (1999). Suicide risk assessment: a review of risk factors for suicide in hundred patients who made severe suicide attempts. Psychosomatics 40:18-27.

Hamilton, N. G. (1986). Positive projective identification. *International Journal of Psychoanalysis* 67:489-496.

Hartmann, E. (1991). *Boundaries in the Mind: A New Psychology of Personality.* New York: Basic Books.

Hartmann, H. (1950). *Essays on Ego Psychology.* New York: International Universities Press.

Hawton, K., Clements, A., Sakarovitch, C., Simkin, S., & Deeks, J.J. (2001). Suicide in doctors: a study of risk according to gender, seniority, and specialty in medical practitioners in England and Wales: 1979-1995. *Journal of Epidemiology and Community Health* 55:296-300.

Hellinga, G., van Luwyn, B., and Dalewijk, H.J. (2000). *Personalities: Master Clinicians Confront the Treatment of Borderline Personality Disorder.* Amsterdam, Holland: Boom Publishers.

Hendin, H., Lipschitz, A., Maltsberger, J.T., et al (2000). Therapists' reactions to patients' suicides. *American Journal of Psychiatry* 157:2022-2027.

Herzog, J. (1984). Fathers and young children: fathering daughters and fathering sons. In: *Foundations of Infant Psychiatry, volume 2,* eds. J.D. Call, E. Galenson, and R. Tyson, pp. 335-343. New York: Basic Books.

Hinsie, L.E. & Campbell, R.J. (1975). *Psychiatric Dictionary.* New York: Oxford University Press.

Hofling, C.K. & Rosenbaum, M. (1986). The extension of credit to patients in psychoanalysis and psychotherapy. In: *The Last Taboo: Money as Symbol and Reality in Psychotherapy and Psychoanalysis,* ed. D.W. Krueger, pp. 202-217. New York: Brunner/Mazel.

Isometsa, E.T., Heikkinen, M.E., Martunen, M.J., et al (1995). The last appointment before suicide: is suicide intent communicated? *American Journal of Psychiatry* 152:919-922.

Jacobs, D. (1986). On negotiating fees with psychotherapy and psychoanalytic patients. In: *The Last Taboo: Money as Symbol and Reality in Psychotherapy and Psychoanalysis,* ed. D.W. Krueger, pp. 121-131. New York: Brunner/Mazel.

Jacobs, D. & Brewer, M. (2004). APA practice guideline provides recommendations for assessing and treating patients with suicidal behaviors. *Psychiatric Annals* 34:373-380.

Jacobson, E. (1964). *The Self and the Object World*. New York: International Universities Press.

Javier, R. A. (1990). The suitability of insight-oriented therapy for the Hispanic poor, and the disadvantaged: application and conceptualization. *Journal of the American Academy of Psychoanalysis* 20:455-476.

Johnson, A.M. & Szurek, S.A. (1952). The genesis of antisocial acting out in children and adults. *Psychoanalytic Quarterly* 21:323-343.

Jones, E. (1913). The God complex. In: *Essays in Applied Psychoanalysis, Vol. II*, pp. 244-265. New York: International Universities Press, 1973.

Jones, E. (1918). Anal erotic character traits. In: *Paper on Psychoanalysis*, pp. 413-437. London: Bailliere, Tindall and Cox, 1950.

Kakar, S. (1985). Psychoanalysis and non-western cultures. *International Review of Psychoanalysis* 12:441-448.

Katan, A. (1961). Some thoughts about the role of verbalization in early childhood. *Psychoanalytic Study of the Child* 16:184-193.

Kaufmann, W. (1976). Some emotional uses of money. In: *The Psychoanalysis of Money*, ed. E. Borneman, pp. 227-252. New York: Urizen Books.

Kernberg, O.F. (1970). A psychoanalytic classification of character pathology. *Journal of the American Psychoanalytic Association* 18:800-822.

Kernberg, O.F. (1975). *Borderline Conditions and Pathological Narcissism*. New York: Jason Aronson.

Kernberg, O.F. (1976). *Object Relations Theory and Clinical Psychoanalysis*. New York: Jason Aronson.

Kernberg, O.F. (1977). Boundaries and structure in love relations. *Journal of the American Psychoanalytic Association* 25:81-114.

Kernberg, O.F. (1980). *Internal World and External Reality*. New York: Jason Aronson.

Kernberg, O.F. (1984). *Severe Personality Disorders: Psychotherapeutic Strategies*. New Haven, CT: Yale University Press.

Kernberg, O.F. (1992). *Aggression in Personality Disorders and Perversions*. New Haven, CT: Yale University Press.

Kernberg, O.F. (1995). *Love Relations, Normality and Pathology*. New Haven, CT: Yale University Press.

Kernberg, O.F., Selzer, M.A., Koenigsberg, H.W., Carr, A.C. & Appelbaum, A.H. (1990). *Psychodynamic Psychotherapy of Borderline Patients*. New York: Basic Books.

Kessler, R.C., Borges, G. & Walters, E.E. (1999). Prevalence of an risk factors for life time suicide attempts in the National Comorbidity Survey. *Archives of General Psychiatry* 56:617-626.

Khan, M.M.R. (1963). The concept of cumulative trauma. *Psychoanalytic Study of the Child* 18:286-306.

Killingmo, B. (1989). Conflict and deficit: implications for technique. *International Journal of Psychoanalysis* 70:65-79.

Klauber, J. (1981). *Difficulties in the Analytic Encounter*. New York: Jason Aronson.

Klein, M. (1935). A contribution to the psychogenesis of manic-depressive states. In: *Love, Guilt and reparation and Other Works 1921-1945*, pp. 248-257. New York: The Free Press, 1975.

Klein, M. (1940). Mourning and its relation to manic-depressive states. In: *Love, Guilt, and Reparation and Other Works, 1921-1945*, pp. 262-289. New York: The Free Press, 1975.

Klein, M. (1946). Notes on some schizoid mechanisms. In: *Envy and Gratitude and Other Works, 1946-1963*, pp. 1-24. New York: The Free Press, 1975.

Knapp, B.L. (2000). *Gambling, Game, and Psyche*. Albany, NY: State University of New York Press.

Kogan, I. (2007). Breaking of boundaries and craving for oneness. In: *Interpersonal Boundaries: Variations and Violations*, ed. S. Akhtar, pp. 61-85. Lanham, MD: Jason Aronson.

Kohut, H. (1977). *The Restoration of the Self*. New York: International Universities Press.

Krueger, D.W. (1986a). *The Last Taboo: Money as Symbol and Reality in Psychotherapy and Psychoanalysis*, ed. D. W. Krueger. New York: Brunner/Mazel.

Krueger, D.W. (1986b). A self-psychological view of money. In: *The Last Taboo: Money as Symbol and Reality in Psychotherapy and Psychoanalysis*, ed. D.W. Krueger, pp. 24-32. New York: Brunner/Mazel.

Lager, E. & Zwerling, I. (1980). Time orientation and psychotherapy in the ghetto. *American Journal of Psychiatry* 137:306-309.

Landis, B. (1970). Ego boundaries. *Psychological Issues Monographs* 6:1-177.

Laplanche, J. & Pontalis, J.B. (1973). *The Language of Psychoanalysis.* New York: W.W. Norton.

Leaff, L. (1991). Separation-individuation and adolescence with special reference to character formation. In *Beyond the Symbiotic Orbit: Advances in Separation Individuation Theory—Essays in the Honor of Selma Kramer,* eds. S. Akhtar and H. Parens, pp.189-208. Hillsdale, N.J: The Analytic Press.

Levine, H. (2005). The sins of fathers: narcissistic boundaries and the power politics of psychoanalysis. Presented at the Fall Meetings of the American Psychoanalytic Association, January 19, 2005.

Lewin, R.A. & Schulz, C. (1992). *Losing and Fusing: Borderline Transitional Object and Self Relations.* Northvale, NJ: Jason Aronson.

Lifson, L. & Geist, R.A. (1999). *The Psychology of Investing.* New York: Wiley.

Limentani, A. (1989). *Between Freud and Klein: The Psychoanalytic Quest for Knowledge and Truth.* London: Free Association Books.

Lion, J.R. & Herschler, J.A. (1998). The stalking of clinicians by their patients. In: *The Psychology of Stalking: Clinical and Forensic Perspectives,* ed. J.R. Meloy, pp. 165-173. San Diego, CA: Academic Press.

Lorand, S. & Console, W. (1958). Therapeutic results in psychoanalytic treatment without fee. *International Journal of Psychoanalysis* 39:59-72.

Lower, R., Escoll, P. & Huxster, H. (1972). Bases for judgments of analyzability. *Journal of the American Psychoanalysis Association* 20:610-621.

Mago, R., Certa, K., Markov, D., & Kunkel, E.J.S. (2004). Suicide risk assessments. *Current Psychiatry* 3:2-6.

Mahler, M.S. (1958). On two crucial phases of integration of the sense of identity: separation-individuation and bisexual identity. *Journal of the American Psychoanalytic Association* 6:136-139.

Mahler, M.S. (1971). A study of the separation-individuation process and its possible application to borderline phenomena in the psychoanalytic situation. *Psychoanalytic Study of the Child* 26:402-424.

Mahler, M.S. (1972). Rapprochement subphase of the separation-individuation process. *Psychoanalytic Quarterly* 41:487-506.

Mahler, M.S., Pine, F., & Bergman, A. (1975). *The Psychological Birth of the Human Infant.* New York: Basic Books.

Maltsberger, J.T. & Buie, D.H. (1974). Countertransference, hate in the treatment of suicidal patients. *Archives of General Psychiatry* 30:625-633.

McCulloch, J.W. & Phillip, A.E. (1972). *Suicidal Behaviour.* New York: Oxford Press.

McManus, J. (2003). *Positively Fifth Street: Murderers, Cheetahs, and Binion's World Series of Poker.* New York: Picador.

Melges, F. T. & Swartz, M.S. (1989). Oscillations of attachment in borderline disorder. *American Journal of Psychiatry* 146:1115-1120.

Menniger, K.A. (1938). *Man Against Himself.* New York: Harcourt.

Menniger, K.A. & Holzman, P.S. (1973). *Theory of Psychoanalytic Technique.* New York: Basic Books.

Milller, J. (1965). On the return of symptoms in the terminal phase of psychoanalysis. *International Journal of Psychoanalysis* 46:487-501.

Modell, A. (1965). On aspects of the superego's development. *International Journal of Psychoanalysis* 46:323-331.

Moore, B.E. & Fine, B.D. (1968). *A Glossary of Psychoanalytic Terms and Concepts.* New York: American Psychoanalytic Association.

Moore, B.E. & Fine, B.D. (1990). *Psychoanalytic Terms and Concepts.* New Haven, CT: Yale University Press.

Mullen, P.E. & Purcell, R. (2007). Stalking of the therapist. In: *Severe Personality Disorders: Everyday Issues in Clinical Practice,* eds. B. van Luyn, S. Akhtar, and W.J. Livesley, pp. 196-210. Cambridge, U.K.: Cambridge University Press.

Niederland, W.G. (1981). The survivor syndrome: further observations and dimensions. *Journal of the American Psychoanalytic Association* 29:413-421.

Olarte, S. & Lenze, R. (1984). Learning to do psychoanalytic therapy with inner city population. *Journal of the American Academy of Psychoanalysis* 12:89-99.

Olsson, P.A. (1986). Complexities in the psychology and psychotherapy of the phenomenally wealthy. In: *The Last Taboo: Money as Symbol and Reality in Psychotherapy and Psychoanalysis,* ed. D.W. Krueger, pp. 55-69. New York: Brunner/Mazel.

Parens, H. (1979). *The Development of Aggression in Early Childhood.* New York: Jason Aronson.

Parens, H. (2006). Why boundaries, fences, and walls around the self? A concluding commentary. In: *Interpersonal Boundaries: Variations and Violations,* ed. S. Akhtar, pp. 99-112. Lanham, MD: Jason Aronson.

Parson, M. (2000). *The Dove that Returns, the Dove that Vanishes: Paradox and Creativity in Psychoanalysis.* London: Routledge.

Pasternak, S. (1986). Psychotherapy fees and therapist training. In: *The Last Taboo: Money as Symbol and Reality in Psychotherapy and Psychoanalysis,* ed. D.W. Krueger, pp. 142-157. New York: Brunnel/Mazel.

Pine, F. (1985). *Developmental Theory and Clinical Process.* New Haven, CT: Yale University Press.

Pine, F. (1997). *Diversity and Direction in Psychoanalytic Technique.* New Haven, CT: Yale University Press.

Poussaint, A. & Alexander, A. (2000). *Lay My Burden Down: Unraveling Suicide and the Mental Health Crisis Among African-American Males.* Boston, MA: Beacon Press.

Rapaport, D. (1951). *Organization and Pathology of Thought.* New York: Columbia University Press.

Reich, W. (1933). *Character Analysis.* Transl. V.R. Carfagno. New York: Farrar, Straus, and Giroux.

Reiser, M. (1971). Psychological issues in training for research in psychiatry. *Journal of Psychiatric Review* 8:531-537.

Roland, A. (1988). *In Search of Self in India and Japan.* Princeton, NJ: Princeton University Press.

Ross, J.M. (1995). The fate of relatives and colleagues in the aftermath of sexual boundary violations. *Journal of the American Psychoanalytic Association* 43:959-961.

Roth, S. (1987). *Psychotherapy: The Art of Wooing Nature.* Northvale, NJ: Jason Aronson.

Rothstein, A. (1982). Analyzability. *International Journal of Psychoanalysis* 63:177-188.

Rothstein, A. (1986). The seduction of money: expression of transference love. *Psychoanalytic Quarterly* 55:296-

Roy, A. (2000). Suicide. In: *Kaplan's & Sadock's Comprehensive Textbook of Psychiatry, Seventh Edition, Volume Two.* Eds. B. Sadock and V. Sadock, pp. 2031-2040. Philadelphia, PA: Lippincott, Williams, & Wilkins.

Ruiz, R. (1981). Cultural and historical perspectives in *Counseling the Culturally Different*, ed. D. Sue, pp. 186-215. New York: John Wiley.

Rycroft, C. (1972). *A Critical Dictionary of Psychoanalysis*. London: Penguin Books.

Sander, L. (1964). Adaptive relationships in early mother-child interaction. *Journal of the American Academy of Child and Adolescent Psychiatry* 3:231-264.

Sander, L. (1983). Polarity, paradox, and the organizing process in development. In: *Frontiers of Infant Psychiatry, Volume II*, eds. J.D. Call, E.D. Galenson, and R. I. Tyson, pp333-346.

Sandler, J. (1960). The background of safety. In: *From Safety to Superego: Selected Papers of Joseph Sandler*, pp. 1-8. New York: Guildford, 1987.

Sandler, J. & Sandler, A.M. (1983). The 'second censorship', the 'three-box model', and some technical implications. *International Journal of Psychoanalysis* 64:413-415.

Schlesinger, H. (2003). *The Texture of Treatment*. Hillsdale, NJ: The Analytic Press.

Schoener, G.R., Milgrom, J.H., Gonsioreck, J.C., Luepker, E.T. & Condroe, R.M. (1989). *Psychotherapists Sexual Involvement with Clients: Intervention and Prevention*. Minneapolis, MN: Walk-In Counseling Center.

Schofield, W. (1964). *Psychotherapy: The Purchase of Friendship*. New York: Prentice-Hall.

Schonbar, R. (1986). The fee as focus of transference and countertransference in treatment. In: *The Last Taboo: Money as Symbol and Reality in Psychotherapy and Psychoanalysis*, ed. D.W. Krueger, pp. 33-47. New York: Brunner/Mazel.

Searles, H.F. (1960). *The Non-Human Environment in Normal Development and Schizophrenia*. New York: International Universities Press.

Searles, H.F. (1967). The 'dedicated physician' in psychotherapy and psychoanalysis. In: *Crosscurrents in Psychiatry & Psychoanalysis*, ed. R.W. Gibson, 128-143. Philadelphia, PA: J.B. Lippincott Company

Seelig, B.J. & Rosof, L.S. (2000). Normal and pathological altruism. *Journal of the American Psychoanalytic Association* 49:933-959.

Selzer, M.A., Koenigsberg, H.W. & Kernberg, O.F. (1987). The initial contract in the treatment of borderline patients. *American Journal of Psychiatry* 144:927-930.

Sholevar, G.P. (1985). Marital assessment. In: *Contemporary Marriage*, ed. D. Goldberg, pp. 290-311. Homewood, IL: Dorsey.

Sholevar, G.P. (1995). Family development and life cycle. In: *Psychiatry, Volume II*, ed. R. Michels, pp. 1-9. Philadelphia, PA: J.B. Lippencott.

Simon, R.I. (2004). Assessing and Managing Suicide Risk: Guidelines for Clinically Based Risk Management. Washington, D.C.: American Psychiatric Publishing, Inc.

Slater, E. & Roth, M. (1977). *Clinical Psychiatry*. London: Bailliere and Tindall.

Spitz, R. (1965). *The First Year of Life*. New York: International Universities Press.

Stack, S. (2004). Suicide risk among physicians: a multivariate analysis. *Archives of Suicide Research* 8:287-292.

Stengel, E. (1964). *Suicide and Attempted Suicide*. Baltimore, MD: Penguin Books.

Stone, M. (1972). Treating the wealthy and their children. *International Journal of Child Psychotherapy* 1:15-46.

Stone, M. (1990). *The Borderline Syndrome*. New York: McGraw-Hill.

Strenger, C. (1989). The classic and romantic visions in psychoanalysis. *International Journal of Psychoanalysis* 70:595-610.

Sue, D. W. & Sue, D. (1977). Barriers to effective cross-cultural counseling. *Journal of Counseling Psychology* 24:420-429.

Tausk, V. (1918). Uber die entstehong des beeinflussungsapparates in der schizophrenie. *International Journal of Psychoanalysis* 5:1-33.

Thomae, H. & Kachele, H. (1994). *Psychoanalytic Practice, Volume 2*. Northvale, NJ: Jason Aronson.

Tyson, P. (2005). Affects, agency, and self-regulation. *Journal of the American Psychoanalytic Association* 53:159-187.

Tyson, P. (2006). Boundary formation in children: normality and pathology. In: *Interpersonal Boundaries: Variations and Violations*, ed. S. Akhtar, pp. 15-28. Lanham, MD: Jason Aronson.

Ursano, R.J., Sonnenberg, S.M., & Lazar, S.G. (1998). *Concise Guide to Psychodynamic Psychotherapy.* Washington, DC: American Psychiatric Press.

Volkan, V.D. (1976). *Primitive Internalized Object Relations.* New York: International Universities Press.

Volkan, V.D. (1988). *The Need to Have Enemies and Allies: From Clinical Practice to International Relationships.* Northvale, NJ: Jason Aronson.

Volkan, V.D. (1997). *Bloodlines: From Ethnic Pride to Ethnic Terrorism.* New York: Straus, Farrer, and Giroux.

Volkan, V.D. & Akhtar, S. (1997). *The Seed of Madness: Constitution, Environment, and Fantasy in the Organization of the Psychotic Core.* Madison, CT: International Universities Press.

Waelder, R. (1936). The principle of multiple function: observations on multiple determination. *Psychoanalytic Quarterly* 5:45-62.

Wahl, C. (1974). Psychoanalysis of the rich, the famous, and the influential. *Contemporary Psychoanalysis* 10:71-85.

Weiss, J.M.A. (1974). Suicide. In: *American Handbook of Psychiatry, Second Edition, Volume III*, eds. S. Arieti and E.B. Brody, pp. 743-765. New York: Basic Books.

Werman, D.S. (1979). Chance, ambiguity, and psychological mindedness. *Psychoanalytic Quarterly* 48:107-115.

Werman, D.S. (1983). Suppression as a defense. *Journal of the American Psychoanalytic Association* 31 (supplement): 405-419.

Wing, L. (1981). Asperger's syndrome: a clinical account. *Psychological Medicine* 11:115-129.

Winnicott, D. W. (1935). The manic defense. In: *Collected Papers: Through Paediatrics to Psychoanalysis*, pp. 129-144. London: Tavistock, 1958.

Winnicott, D. W. (1953). Transitional objects and transitional phenomena: a study of the first not-me possession. *International Journal of Psychoanalysis* 34:89-97.

Winnicott, D. W. (1956). The antisocial tendency. In: *Collected Papers: Through Paediatrics to Psychoanalysis*, pp.300-306. New York: Basic Books.

Winnicott, D. W. (1960). Ego dissociation in terms of true and false self. In: *The Maturational Processes and the Facilitating Environment*, pp. 140-152. New York: International Universities Press, 1965.

Winnicott, D. W. (1965). *The Maturational Processes and the Facilitating Environment*. New York: International Universities Press.

Winnicott, D. W. (1969). The mother-infant experience of mutuality. In: *Psychoanalytic Explorations*, ed. C. Winnicott, R. Shephard, and M. Davis, pp. 251-260. Cambridge, MA: Harvard University Press, 1989.

Winnicott, D. W. (1971). *Playing and Reality*. London: Penguin Books.

Wolf, E. (1993). Selfobject experience: development, psychopathology, treatment. In: *Mahler and Kohut: Perspectives on Development, Psychopathology, and Technique*, eds. S. Kramer and S. Akhtar, pp. 65-96. Northvale, NJ: Jason Aronson.

Wolpert, E.A. (1980). Major affective disorders. In: *Comprehensive Textbook of Psychiatry (Third Edition), Vol. II*, eds. H.I. Kaplan, A.M. Freedman, and B.J. Sadock, pp. 1319-1331. Baltimore, MD: Williams and Wilkins Company.

Wright, K. (1991). *Vision and Separation: Between Mother and Baby*. Northvale, NJ: Jason Aronson.

Zimmerman, D. (1982). Analyzability in relation to early psychopathology. *International Journal of Psychoanalysis* 63:189-200.

169